NEW BEGINNINGS:
ISSUES AND NEEDS IN INTERNATIONAL KINSHIP CARE

NEW BEGINNINGS:
ISSUES AND NEEDS IN INTERNATIONAL KINSHIP CARE

KLAUS SERR & DAVID ROSE

Australian Scholarly

First published 2016 by
Australian Scholarly Publishing Pty Ltd
7 Lt Lothian St Nth, North Melbourne, Victoria 3051
tel 03 9329 696 / *fax* 03 9329 5452
aspic@ozemail.com / www.scholarly.info

ISBN: 978-1-925333-49-7

To Feray Ergun
With many thanks and best wishes

CONTENTS

Foreword

by The Honourable Alastair Nicholson AO RFD QC

As Patron of International Social Service Australia I am honoured to be asked to write a short foreword for this excellent publication. It is based on a study that was led by Klaus Serr at ISS Australia and conducted in collaboration with the Department of Social Work at the University of Melbourne.

This work sheds an important light on a little known aspect of Australia's migration program; namely the specific needs, support requirements and particular service responses of those children and young people who arrive in Australia on orphan relative visas and the family members who become their carers. The work makes it clear that all need much more support than is presently available and that they face considerable additional challenges. Carer families are often themselves comparatively recent arrivals in Australia, are facing the challenges of integrating into a new and alien society, are often poor and living in less than optimum housing, and already have large families of their own.

They have often come from the same conflict zones as the orphan children for whom they care, and face additional problems caused by the xenophobia and fear promoted by some ignorant and racist members of the Australian community towards people from other countries who have a different culture and religion to the mainstream.

Orphan children and young people face the additional problem of having lost their parents, often in horrendous circumstances, and have had to face the difficulties of life in refugee camps and the tortuous process of negotiating our bureaucratic and increasingly uncaring and militaristic immigration system.

I am impressed with the study's finding that there is not only a significant need for specialised support services to assist during the resettlement process, but that assessment should not play a major role in this process. Of course, all children and young persons should be protected from abuse, but the usual tests are clearly inappropriate in an emergency situation. Their removal to the care of people with whom they have had no previous connection would be extremely traumatic.

There has been a considerable increase in the number of orphans entering Australia on these visas, and there are strong humanitarian and practical reasons why their number should continue to increase.

Australians who oppose any such increase and expenditure or support of such orphans and their carers fail to recognise the enormous contribution to this country made by people who have come here in similar circumstances in the past.

The Honourable Alastair Nicholson AO RFD QC

PREFACE

by Professor Marie Connolly, The University of Melbourne

Throughout history and across cultures families have looked after children within their kinship systems. Extended families have provided essential care for children, from basic childcare for busy parents, to the raising of orphaned children. This elemental expression of relationship and commitment to caring provides a foundational safety net for children who are unable to live with their parents.

Over the past twenty years there has been an important shift in Australia toward the use of extended family systems to support and care for vulnerable children. Australia has increasingly come to rely upon family members to care for their more vulnerable relatives due to the recognition that the developmental, cultural and spiritual needs of children can best be met within families. Yet we have paid relatively little attention to the nature and scope of the caregiving activities of extended family. Indeed, fairly scant attention has been paid to this substantial and growing population internationally, leaving Australia with very little information on how to effectively utilize and support traditional extended family support to achieve better outcomes for vulnerable children.

In general, research into kinship care has not kept pace with its growth as the preferred placement option for children who cannot live with their parents. It is pleasing therefore to see this research that examines the issues and support needs of children and young people who arrive in Australia on 'orphan relative' visas, and also the needs of the relatives here who agree to become their carers. Perhaps not surprisingly these children and carers share many of the issues confronting other kinship carers. Research suggests that kinship carers face physical and socio-economic difficulties that can impact on their capacity to provide care (Beotto 2010; Dunne and Kettler 2008; Breman 2014), and they often have poor access to services (Wichinsky et al 2013). Caregivers also report feelings of isolation (Strozier 2012) and are frequently left to 'fend for themselves' when they need professional support (Brown and Sen 2014). Children who move into kinship care arrangements can also experience complex problems (Tarren-Sweeney 2013) resulting in a need for well supported care. They may experience poor mental health or significant trauma. Caregivers and practitioners need to both understand the issues that these children bring, and be able to respond in ways that will support better outcomes for them.

Much has been written about the need for greater responsiveness toward vulnerable children and their kinship carers. It is important that we also understand the particular needs of children who come to Australia as orphans, and the issues that their kinship carers face. It is clear from this report that while they share many of the same issues as other kinship carers, they also have additional needs and service requirements that reflect their particular family situation and experience. This report is an important exploration of these unique family circumstances, providing us with critical insights into how we might address them.

Professor Marie Connolly
The University of Melbourne

ACKNOWLEDGMENTS

This study received generous support from the Barr Family Foundation.

The authors also gratefully acknowledge the numerous contributions made by the many people supporting the research and this publication. We especially acknowledge:

- All research participants who generously gave their time. Many thanks to all those who commented on the initial findings and discussed them with us.
- Heeral Sanghvi, an RMIT social work student who undertook her field work with the project. She did much more than could ever have been expected, was a delight to work with and kept us all sane when the going was tough. Heeral also continued supporting the project as a volunteer, for some time after completing her placement, which was greatly appreciated.
- Staff at International Social Service (ISS) Australia, particularly Fionn Skiotis for his personal and organisational assistance, and also Syd Balachandran, Ann Freilich, Damon Martin, Ann Wollner, Siobhan Kavanagh and others for their interest and support. Special thanks to Helen Freris who assisted in many ways, read and discussed various parts of the findings and also made valuable comments on the final manuscript. Special gratitude to Feray Ergun who had input into all stages of the research, made valuable editorial suggestions and was enormously supportive throughout the entire process. The authors and ISS Australia wish to dedicate this study to Feray, not only for her generous assistance and support, but also to pay tribute to her work and commitment to ISS Australia over the past eight years. We wish her well for the future.
- Staff at the University of Melbourne, especially Marie Connolly who assisted and supported us in various ways and was kind enough to write the foreword.
- Australian Scholarly Publishing (ASP), especially Nick Walker for his

interest in publishing this study and the ASP team for their continuing advice and support.

- Thanks to Toby who took an interest in the project, read parts of the manuscript and assisted in various ways.

Special thanks to Eric Porter, whose reviewing and editing of the manuscript was greatly appreciated.

List of Boxes and Tables

List of boxes

List of tables

EXECUTIVE SUMMARY

> If you put the correct intervention in place early on, in a timely manner, in our experience at least 80% of orphans have succeeded. They have completed their [educational] courses, are employed in meaningful jobs and have become productive members of society and have a lot to give (Professional 8).

This study examines the issues, needs, support requirements and future service responses for children and young people who arrive in Australia on Orphan Relative Visas and the relatives who agree to become their carers. This is an expanding group of children in out-of-home care. The fact that they migrate to Australia, often from conflict zones and have frequently suffered major trauma and loss means that they present with unique and acute needs.

Once in Australia, these children acquire permanent residency via the Orphan Relative Visa or the Remaining Relative Visa and reside in the care of family members other than their parents. These visas are part of the Family Migration Stream, permanent visas which allow children to live in Australia indefinitely. The Orphan Relative Visa has two subclasses: 1) Subclass 117 is for offshore applications where children are in another country, and 2) Subclass 837 is for onshore applications for children already in Australia on another visa. In recent years there has been a steady increase in the use of these visas. For example, over the decade to 30 June 2012, 2,759 children and young people arrived in Australia on the Orphan Relative Visa and a large number settled in Victoria, New South Wales and Queensland (Department of Immigration and Citizenship, 2013). Most recently, in the 12 months from 1 July 2013 to 30 June 2014, 458 Orphan Relative Visa holders arrived in Australia (Australian Government, 2014).

This study is based on the views of professionals experienced in working with Orphan Relative Visa holders and their kinship carers in Australia. These views were collected through semi-structured interviews and built on two previous studies into the Orphan Relative Visa process conducted by ISS Australia (Kavanagh, 2011; 2013).

Findings

Overall, the study found that orphan children and young people and their relative carers in Australia experience similar issues and needs to other families involved in kinship care arrangements. In addition, they face a number of complexities and challenges due to pre-arrival experiences and the international migration process. Given the increasing number of Orphan Relative Visa holders migrating to Australia to live with relatives, often from conflict zones with significant trauma histories, there is a need for specialised support services to assist during the resettlement process. Although there are differing views as to the degree to which such support services should also have an assessment role, particularly in relation to suitability of the kinship care placement, the major view of professionals in this study was that the service should primarily be an ongoing support and information service to aid the resettlement process, with the capacity to link to and engage with other community services and supports where required.

Participants felt that the resettlement of orphans entering Australia via the Orphan Relative Visa process is an important humanitarian responsibility of the nation and they support the continuation of this programme. Many informants therefore suggest an increase in Australia's annual intake of orphans, as more people become displaced around the world. Most participants also think that orphan placements have been reasonably successful, despite the fact that resettlement is not an easy process for either carers or orphans. In general, orphans are viewed as a resource for the country and early support will increase the likelihood of their successful re-settlement experience and future productive citizenship.

Overall recommendations:

Based on the findings and key conclusions drawn from this study, the following overall recommendations are made:

1. That there be greater recognition of the issues and needs of Orphan Relative Visa holders and their carers in government policy and associated service provision.

2. That service provision and support services for Orphan Relative Visa

holders and their carers should recognise the specific support needs related to the international displacement and migration process and subsequent settlement issues in Australia.

3. That a specific support service for Orphan Relative Visa holders and their carers be funded, and established in one or more non-government organisations with the capacity to provide culturally appropriate family support and case management services.

That the orientation of support services established for the Orphan Relative Visa program primarily be support and resourcing functions to maximise the likelihood that placements will continue rather than services being focussed primarily on assessing suitability and managing risk.

1. Introduction

The focus of this study is an expanding group of children in out-of-home care, namely those who reside in the care of family members other than their parents, and who have acquired permanent residency in Australia via the Orphan Relative Visa or the Remaining Relative Visa. These visas are part of the Family Migration Stream, permanent visas which allow children to live in Australia indefinitely. The Orphan Relative Visa has two subclasses: 1) Subclass 117 is for offshore applications where children are in another country, and 2) Subclass 837 is for onshore applications for children already in Australia on another visa.

Holders of this visa can be divided into two groups: the first and larger group is comprised of children who, through displacement, conflict or other humanitarian crisis in their countries of origin, have lost their parents; they are subsequently sponsored to live in Australia by a family member already settled in this country. The smaller group of children on the Orphan Relative Visa category have been removed from their parents by a statutory child protection authority and, after appropriate assessments of their Australian resident family members, are placed in their care by order of a Court.

This latter group mostly originate from the United Kingdom or another industrialised country with a well-developed child protection system and able to facilitate the assessment of international family members as kinship carers. In both instances, the sponsor of a child must be an Australian citizen or Australian permanent resident who is at least 18 years of age. Normally they must have been settled in Australia for at least two years and be either a sibling, 'a grandparent, aunt, uncle, niece, nephew (or step equivalent)' who can demonstrate that they can provide parental responsibility for the children (Department of Immigration and Border Protection, 2014). The common theme uniting these two groups of children is their entry into Australia to live in what may be termed international kinship care. The two groups have specific needs, based on their pre-arrival experiences and post-arrival support needs.

In recent years there has been a steady increase in the use of this visa. For example, over the last decade to 30 June 2012, 2,759 children and young people arrived in Australia on the Orphan Relative Visa, most settling in Victoria, New South Wales and Queensland (Department of Immigration and Citizenship (2013). Most recently in the 12 months from 1 July 2013 to 30 June 2014, 458 Orphan Relative Visa holders arrived in Australia (Australian Government, 2014). Orphan Relative Visa holders come from a wide range of countries and situations. Many of these children and young people were born in countries affected by conflict and displacement, including Afghanistan, Ethiopia, Sudan and Somalia, and may have additional vulnerabilities caused by their experiences during the conflict. International kinship care placements are a big adjustment for carers and children, and families may require support to manage the transition.

This study was conducted by ISS Australia in collaboration with the Department of Social Work at The University of Melbourne and received generous support of the Barr Family Foundation. ISS Australia is a non-government organisation with over 50 years' experience in defending children and connecting families across the world through the provision of professional intercountry social work and legal services. The agency provides intercountry child welfare services, including kinship placement assessments, social work and legal support for international parental child abduction cases, family mediation and post-adoption and general family tracing, counselling and family reunification. ISS Australia is part of the worldwide ISS network which works to protect and support children and families in cross-border situations.

2. Literature Review

This section discusses key literature that has informed this study. A selected overview of the general out-of-home-care and kinship care literature is provided followed by a discussion of the literature on international kinship care which is the focus of the study.

In the Australian context, out-of-home-care refers to arrangements made for children and young people who are unable to live at home because of abuse, neglect or other reasons, and includes residential care, family group homes, and home-based care (incorporating relative or kinship care and standard foster care) (AIHW, 2015; Boetto, 2010). Kinship care can be defined as '…the care provided by relatives or a member of a child's social network when a child cannot live with their parents' (Victorian Department of Human Services, 2009, p. 2). International kinship care is the process whereby the child or young person is required to migrate to another country to be cared for by relatives (Kavanagh, 2013). Kinship care arrangements tend to be less formal than other foster care arrangements but can be categorised as either formal kinship care (where the arrangement has been made or sanctioned by child welfare and/or other authorities) and informal kinship care (where the arrangements have been made informally between family members) (Roby, 2011; Boetto, 2010).

Out of home care and kinship care

The number of children living in out-of-home-care has been increasing in all Australian jurisdictions with 43,009 children in out of home care at 30 June 2014 (a rate of 8.1 per 1,000 children compared to a rate of 7.1 per 1,000 children in 2010) (AIHW, 2015). In Australia kinship care has now become the main type of out-of-home-care arrangement, although the proportion of kinship care to other foster care varies considerably across the different states and territories. At 30 June 2014, 93% of children in out-of-home-care were in home-based type care, with kinship care arrangements at 49% having overtaken other foster care at 41% (AIHW, 2015).

The trend towards increasing rates of kinship/relative care as a proportion of out-of-home-care arrangements has been observed in a growing number of countries, along with increasing attention to the relative risks and benefits of kinship care versus other types of out-of-home-care (Valle & Bravo, 2013; Farmer, 2010; Palacious & Jimenez, 2009). However, a Cochrane Collaboration systematic review of 102 quasi-experimental studies reported in the literature to 2011 compared kinship care to other forms of foster care and found overall kinship foster care was associated with fewer behavioural problems, fewer mental health disorders and better well-being in children compared to non-kinship foster care. Overall, the authors concluded that the review supported the use of kinship foster care as a viable option for out-of-home-care but also noted the methodological limitations of the research currently available (Winokur, Holtan, & Batchelder, 2014).

While the evidence on outcomes for children and young people in kinship care is favourable compared to other forms of care, research has identified a range of issues for kinship carers and the children and young people in kinship care. Some of the potential benefits of kinship care noted in the literature include:

- A stronger sense of belonging and connection to extended family relationships;
- Increased capacity to maintain individual and cultural identity;
- Reduced stigma associated with kinship care compared to other forms of foster care;
- Reduced trauma associated with the separation from parents;
- Enhanced stability of kinship care arrangements and likely longer term placements compared to other forms of foster care which are often characterised by frequent changes in the foster care family (Breman 2014; Boetto 2010; Paxman, 2006; Queensland Child Safety Services, undated).

Conversely, kinship care is not without significant issues, particularly in relation to the impact on the kinship carers. International comparisons have shown that kinship carers tend to be older, female and single and often with lower education and a lower socio-economic status than other foster carers

(Boetto, 2010; Paxman, 2006). The experience of kinship care also often brings a range of problems for the kinship carer and the carer's family, including:

- Significant financial difficulties and associated problems including overcrowded housing, reduced capacity for paid employment and thus more reliance on welfare benefits and the extra direct costs of raising the child or young person, particularly where kinship care arrangements are not supported financially to the same extent as other foster care.
- The direct personal impacts on the kinship carer including poor physical and mental health, fatigue, and loss of independence as well as the need to deal with new family dynamics presented by a new child in the family together with feelings of guilt about what has happened to the child's direct family of origin and the carer's perceived responsibilities to the parents.
- A range of issues related to managing the child's behaviours, addressing any specific needs they have, supporting their participation in educational activities and, depending on the child's situation, also dealing with other support services (Breman, 2014; Boetto, 2010; Paxman, 2006, Yardley, Mason & Watson, 2009).

An international overview of trends in out-of-home-care noted that the observed increase in the proportion of kinship care arrangements within the broader foster care type of out-of-home-care, presents particular challenges for governments and the community to provide the best financial and other direct support for families and individuals who take on the kinship carer role (Valle & Bravo, 2013).

Assessing the suitability of carers is increasingly recognised as a vexed issue. Taking on a foster child or young person can be very difficult, and the availability of additional support is also a factor. It is noted that in the case of formal kinship care arrangements the rigour of assessment of suitability of the carers is often less than in other forms of foster care and in the case of informal kinship care often no assessment of suitability is undertaken at all

(Boetto, 2010; Palacious & Jimenez, 2009). On the one hand, there is an acknowledgement that in some circumstances a kinship care arrangement might present a risk for children if not properly assessed, while on the other hand kinship care does present particular challenges for investigation/assessment of suitability compared to standard processes of foster carer selection. Kinship care arrangements often come about through significant family trauma, are required to take place urgently and, when assessments are done, they often take place after the child or young person is already with their kin. As O'Brien (2013, p.356) suggests:

> While relatives trying to help their extended family can appreciate the agency's need to ensure safety, an extended investigation/assessment process can be an unwelcome, incomprehensible, intrusive and worrying intervention while they are adapting to the difficult task and changes involved in caring for their vulnerable relative.

It is also noted that while kinship carers may see assessments as unwelcome intrusions, when assessment processes are framed in a more positive way they can be a catalyst for bringing needed support services to the carers (Boetto, 2010). There continues to be some tension around the issues of risk versus support in kinship care and whether placement assessments for kinship care should be at the same level of rigour as those for other foster care placements. Further, it is also recognised that many kinship care arrangements are informal and this further complicates the issue of how best to formalise risk and supportive functions.

Australia, like some other countries, has developed a set of standards to guide the provision of out-of-home-care and the overarching principles of these standards are presented in Box 1. It is important to recognise that these principles are intended to apply to all children in out-of-home-care including children in kinship care. Though these principles should also apply to children involved in international kinship care who arrive in Australia on Orphan Relative Visas, there is much less clarity about the experience of this group of children and young people and their kinship carers. The next part of this review will focus on the specific issues of international kinship care.

Box 1: Overarching principles of the national standards for out-of-home-care (2011)

- Children and young people in out-of-home care have their rights respected and are treated in accordance with the United Nations Convention on the Rights of the Child.
- Care provided to children and young people living in out-of-home care is focused on providing a nurturing environment, promoting their best interests, and maximising their potential.
- Children and young people living in out-of-home care are provided with opportunities for their voice to be heard and respected and have the right to clear and consistent information about the reasons for being in care.
- Care provided to children and young people will promote the benefits of ongoing safe, meaningful and positive connection and involvement of parents and families and communities of origin.
- Carers and their families are key stakeholders and partners in the care of children and young people, and their role is to be respected and supported.
- Children and young people living in out-of-home care are provided with a level of quality care that addresses their particular needs and improves their life outcomes.
- Continuous system improvements are designed to achieve better outcomes for all children and young people living in out-of-home care.
- Out-of-home care for children and young people is measured, monitored and reported in a transparent, efficient and consistent manner over time.
- Aboriginal and Torres Strait Islander communities are to be involved in decisions in accordance with the Aboriginal Child Placement Principle.

Source: Department of Families, Housing, Community Services and Indigenous Affairs, 2011, p. 6

International kinship care

An extensive international search through journal papers and grey literature yielded only a very small number of publications dealing with the issues of international kinship care and even fewer on the specific situation of orphans involved in international kinship care. As already noted, international kinship care for orphans has been increasing in Australia and, as the transnational movement of people grows, this trend is likely to continue. The limited literature confirms that little is known about the specific needs and issues of children and carers involved in these international kinship arrangements.

ISS USA has undertaken research examining the barriers to securing international kinship care placements in the USA for children who are in care primarily because of abuse and neglect. The research indicates that despite transnational movements of people and significant waves of immigration into the USA, international relative/kinship care arrangements are under-utilised because, among a range of factors, people are not aware of the option or they hold child safety/risk concerns (Northcott, & Jeffries, 2012). Similarly, another ISS USA linked discussion that mostly focuses on the international options for children in care due to protective concerns, highlights other perceived barriers to international placements including the great cost of arranging and implementing international kinship placements and perceived concerns about the impact on children that often move away from family/friendship networks in the country of origin (Naughton & Fay, 2003). These barriers to implementing successful international kinship care placements in child protection contexts are repeated in other US research (Cardoso, Gomez, & Padilla, 2009; Freundlich, Heffernan, & Jacobs, 2004). Oien (2006) researched informal kinship care networks in Angola and Portugal finding that Angolan children are often sent to live with relatives in Portugal in kinship care arrangements. She notes that while this is generally seen as providing better opportunities for children, the potential for mistreatment and exploitation of children in the new country must also be recognised.

Children and Families Across Borders (CFAB) in the UK has recently conducted research examining international kinship care including a case audit of 101 kinship care cases referred to the agency between 2007 and 2010 and an examination of long-term outcomes for a small sample (n=9) of children in kinship care outside of the UK (Wilson, Enawalla, & Navey, 2014). The case audit revealed potential placements had been explored in 43 countries demonstrating the global nature of the issue and that 30% of the cases were actually placed in another country with kinship carers. While the sample for the long-term follow-up was small, eight of the nine placements had continued indicating that placement stability was good, that children were accessing education and supports, but that the support for the kinship carers was mixed.

In Australia, research on the issue of international kinship care has been limited and most has been conducted by ISS Australia on the issues for children and young people arriving in Australia on Orphan Relative Visas (Kavanagh 2011; 2013). The 2013 study, on which this current work builds, was one of the first to examine the issues for the Orphan Relative Visa group. The research drew on desk-based research and consultations with a small number of professionals and included an analysis of arrivals of Orphan Relative Visa holders in Australia over the decade to 2012. During that period 2,483 children arrived in Australia on Orphan Relative Visas. The data also indicated that the annual rate of arrivals was gradually increasing and that children were often coming from countries enmeshed in war and conflict. Children from these countries had often arrived with little formal assessment or involvement from child welfare authorities in the country of origin or in Australia, and a key issue identified was the extent to which more formalised assessment and support should be provided to the children and their kinship carers in Australia (Kavanagh, 2013).

Conclusions from the literature

This review of the literature confirms kinship care arrangements are increasingly becoming the preferred model of foster care in many countries around the world, and in Australia it has become the most frequently used type of out-of-home-care. The evidence base confirms the outcomes for children in kinship care arrangements are often better than for other types of out-of-home care, and that there are a number of potential advantages for children and young people being placed with relatives when they are unable to live with their parents. However, a number of potential problems for the children/young people and their kinship carers have also been identified. Furthermore, tensions and debates continue around how best to assess the suitability of kinship carers and how carers can best be supported in their role, recognising that substantial numbers of children and young people live in informal kinship care arrangements with little or no connection with child welfare authorities. In relation to international kinship care, the review confirms the relative lack of knowledge and research into the particular circumstances of children and young people who move across borders to be cared for by relatives. While there is a very limited literature confirming the barriers that reduce the capacity to provide international kinship placements as an option for children in care, little has been documented on the experiences of children and their carers once international kinship placements take place. In particular, the experiences of orphans (in comparison to children requiring placements due to child protection concerns) have received very little attention with the exception of previous research by ISS Australia.

3. METHOD

The overall aim of this research was to gain a better understanding of the needs both of orphans on Orphans Relative Visa living in out-of-home-care in Australia and of their carers. To achieve this aim the project employed qualitative methods, consisting of semi-structured interviews with professional key informants. The key informants are referred to throughout this report as the 'Professionals'.

A purposive sampling method was utilised whereby ISS Australia identified key professionals known to have experience working with Orphan Relative Visa children and young people and/or their kinship carers. These professionals were then contacted, provided with information on the study and invited to participate in an interview. The interviews were conducted in-person during the first half of 2015. The duration of the interviews was between 60 to 90 minutes and all were digitally recorded and transcribed in full. The interview schedule consisted of four main questions:

1. What are the issues affecting carers and orphan children/young people?
2. What are the needs of carers and orphan children/young people?
3. What kind of support do carers/orphan children/young people need?
4. How can the current system dealing with Orphan Relative Visas be improved?

Following transcription, the interview transcripts were analysed using thematic analysis to identify themes and issues from the data within four broad categories linked to the interview questions (Bryman, 2008).

Overall, fifteen professionals were interviewed. They were drawn from the government and non-government sector from a range of disciplines and professional contexts, which included: community workers (2); lawyers (1); nurses (2); psychologists (1); social workers (5); teachers (3) and youth workers (1). Their professional expertise, experience and responsibilities included the following areas: adoption/international casework; kinship care/child protection; refugee resettlement, migration/family law; community health care, secondary education/language school system. Interviewees worked in direct practice, management and policy and research positions.

The study was subject to ethical review and approval by The University of Melbourne Human Research Ethics Committee (No. 1442981.1).

4. Findings

This section presents the findings of the study based on the interviews with the professionals. Overall, participants felt that the resettlement of orphans entering Australia via the Orphan Relative Visa process is an important national humanitarian responsibility and they support the continuation of this programme. Many informants suggest an increase in Australia's annual intake of orphans, as more people become displaced around the world.

The presentation of findings in the following sections is arranged in the order of the four key questions asked to all professionals who participated in the study:

1. What are the issues affecting carers and orphan children/young people?
2. What are the needs of carers and orphan children/young people?
3. What kind of support do carers/orphan children/young people need?
4. How can the current system dealing with Orphan Relative Visas be improved?

Each section begins by summarising the commonalities between the two groups, followed by material specifically related to the carers and then the orphans.

Most participants said that orphan placements have been reasonably successful, despite the fact that resettlement is not an easy process for either carers or orphans. Nevertheless, being asked to articulate the issues, needs and support requirements of both carers and orphans, the informants presented a complex picture of multiple concerns that may affect these two groups. After thus first identifying relevant matters under each question area, informants made a constructive contribution particularly in the last section, where they suggested improvements to the current system.

4.1 Issues affecting carers and orphans

> I have worked with these kids and know what they have [and had] to deal with. They have experienced so much loss and pain and most of them have survived enormous adversity. I suppose and have an under-

> standing [of adversity] and compassion. They can be really good in helping industries ... They have a very strong sense of community, are not very individualist and want to make a contribution [in society]. They are giving, sharing and helping and very motivated; they are hardworking, energetic, resilient [and] have lots of life experience (Professional 4).

After data analysis six broad issues emerged. As Box 2 shows they include: insufficient financial and other resources; inadequate accommodation; emotional/psychological issues; cultural complexities and resettlement issues.

Insufficient financial and other resources

According to many informants, financial pressures on carers/host families increase after the arrival of the orphan(s) in the country. In this context it was pointed out that while the Orphan Relative Visa gives orphans permanent residency status and access to the Medicare system in Australia, orphans are ineligible for Centrelink benefits for at least two years. This then places the financial responsibility onto the carers, many of whom may have signed a contractual agreement with the government to support the orphans after arrival.

Box 2: Potential issues

Common to both Groups

Financial/other resources

- Lack of adequate financial and other resources
- Inability, at times, to meet various competing needs

Accommodation

- Lack of living and sleeping space
- Possible over crowding
- Lack of privacy

Preparation

- Unprepared for the re-settlement experience
- Unrealistic expectations of each other

Culture

- Potential culture shock
- Misunderstandings
- Misinterpreting actions and behaviour

Emotional/psychological

- Potential family conflict due to additional stresses
- Potential adjustment difficulties

Legal

- Lack of general system knowledge and how Australian law may apply in various situations
- Uncertainty about rights and obligations

Carer Specific

- Difficulties in navigating immigration system and meeting visa requirements
- Difficulties accessing services/resources
- Problems in coping with additional stresses (spouse, biological children etc.)
- Potential difficulties with biological children
- Lack of:
  - information/knowledge of welfare system
  - sufficient financial and other resources to care for extra person(s) and/or to meet all needs of orphans/members of host family
  - skills to deal with behavioural issues
  - understanding of orphan experiences and their needs

Orphan Specific

- Potential exposure to racism
- Past trauma, grief and loss
- Difficulties in fitting into the new life
- Lack of social engagement

Financial impact

A number of participants stated that in their experience, carers often come from a lower socio-economic background. This may make their ability to support themselves, their families and the new arrival(s) even more difficult than it already is (also see Financial/resource needs in section 4.2). Other informants suggest that additional financial stress depends on the number of orphans actually arriving (needing support), what they expect/how demanding they are, whether the carer is employed or on Centrelink benefits and whether the carer has other children and a family of their own.

In general, the arrival of the orphan(s) means:

- A decrease in financial and other resources due to additional commitments
- An exaggeration of existing financial difficulties
- A potential increase in financial stress that could lead to other difficulties (e.g. in areas such as housing, health care, etc.).

One example of this was the inability of carers and orphans to access specialist services that offer emotional and psychological support, as pointed out by Professional 8 (see Box 3).

Box 3: Lack of financial resources to deal with emotional issues
Most psychologists do not use interpreters or bulk bill and therefore those who need it cannot afford [additional costs] for each session. Most people are not even aware they are entitled to these sessions or that they need it and would only know if the agency they are working with identify. Psychologists may not be culturally competent and may not have any understanding what the kids have been through and are not familiar with the issues (Professional 8).

The impact of a lack of adequate resources has a number of implications and affects both groups.

For the carers it often means that:

- Despite the possibility of some extra assistance from Centrelink, financial and other resources available to care for extra person(s) and/or to meet all needs of every member of the host family will be insufficient
- Some carers may be heavily in debt to other people in their respective communities who may have helped/lent them money to assist with bringing the orphan(s) to Australia
- To cover additional expenses involved, a carer may need to work extra hours which can increase stress levels and difficulties associated with care and other household/relationship arrangements
- Potential family conflict (spouse, children) over things that are un-

available or seen as unreasonable requests from orphan(s)

- Possible hostility from biological child/children if orphan(s) perceived to receive preferential treatment.

For the orphan(s) it often means:

- Available financial and other resources may be insufficient to meet all their needs/expectations
- Being financially dependent on carer/host family for a considerable period of time
- Feelings of dependency/lack of independence
- Frustrations at not having their expectations fulfilled
- Possible embarrassment at inability to keep up with their peer group/friends
- Coming under pressure to leave school early to find work and support themselves or carer/host family
- Possible conflict with members of the host family through competition for scarce resources
- Increased risk for young adult orphans of homelessness and/or involvement with the criminal justice system.

Inadequate accommodation

Most key informants emphasise the important role housing plays in the well-being of individuals/families. For many professionals, accommodation is crucial in individual and family stability, providing not only the necessary shelter but also a place of belonging, recreation and safety. Professional 11, for example, describes some of the difficulties when accommodation is not sufficient:

> Houses might be run down, phone won't be connected, young people don't have mobiles and can't afford to get one ... There might be tensions in the house which cause people to spend a lot of time away from

> their homes. Worst case scenarios could also see mixed gender people sharing rooms which may not be appropriate in a lot of circumstances. Lack of privacy would be an issue, there could be a feeling that they are just not welcome in that space and young people are reporting feeling that they're going home and not feeling like a part of that unit and feel like a burden, feel like they are in someone else's space and they'd like to move. It's hard to clean a crowded house too (Professional 11).

A lack of adequate accommodation affects both groups after the arrival of the orphans. There is also a specific impact on each group in relation to the orphans, as examples in Box 4 highlight.

Thus, the arrival of the orphans has various effects and the general impact is seen as:

- Lack of culturally appropriate housing that caters for cultural needs and for sharing with potentially large families
- Increased pressure on existing living and sleeping spaces/resources
- Possible overcrowding
- Decrease of privacy and personal spaces
- Financial inability to move into larger accommodation.

For the carers it often means:

- Less space to have time alone and time out
- Fewer opportunities to reflect and recuperate
- Inadequate space for recreational activities/hobbies at home
- Insufficient private space for existing family relationships
- Lack of space to meet people/friends.

Box 4: Orphans' precarious sleeping arrangements

In many cases accommodation is not adequate with little space available. Sometimes there isn't even a bed and the orphan may be asked to share [it] with other children, or sleep on the couch. But when the kids come, they don't want to share the bed with anyone. While it is okay to share the same room, the orphan and the carer's kids may not understand or get on with each other … Girls might also be scared in the new family, with male members of the family and there is potential of sexual abuse. While the abuser may threaten the victim not to reveal the abuse so that the orphan might be scared and frightened, there might be a lot of shame associated with having been abused, so that the girl would find it difficult to reveal and tell someone to get assistance (Professional 14).

Often there is not enough space in the house and sometimes there are five children in one bedroom with mattresses on the floor, or perhaps two kids in one bed (Professional 7).

The orphans often share a room with the carer's younger children, which is not always appropriate due to different genders and age groups. Teenagers require privacy and tension can sometimes surface and erupt (Professional 5).

For the orphan(s) it often means:

- Insufficient private space to develop independence and a sense of belonging
- Having the feeling of living in someone else's home rather than in their own
- A lack of room/space to study
- A lack of space to meet people, develop friendships
- A lack of private sleeping arrangements, having own bedroom, feeling uncomfortable sharing bedroom with others such as the biological child/children of the carer (as illustrated in Box 4).

Emotional/psychological issues

> Emotional issues can arise from previous (pre migration) experiences plus settlement (Professional 8).

Many informants note the potential emotional and psychological distress both carers and orphans are likely to experience before and after the orphan(s) settle(s) in Australia. This was said to affect both groups in general terms and through the impact it has on each group in various ways (see Boxes 5 and 6, for instance).

A number of general issues were thus identified, affecting both groups. These included:

- Grief and loss issues due to past experiences
- Anxiety due to new situations, experiences and expectations
- Stress due to length/difficulties about the visa process and having to deal with authorities
- Increased stress/anxiety after settlement
- Adjustment problems to new situation and systems.

Issues specifically for carers

As demonstrated below, issues that impact on carers are varied. One example of this is shown in Box 5, where a young carer found it difficult to cope with the added and unexpected responsibilities of looking after two orphans.

Box 5: Case example
A young refugee man in his early 20s, living in Australia, was joined by an older sister on a medical visa for medical treatment who brought her two young children with her. The sister subsequently died and the young brother who was left behind was forced into accepting the care of his sisters' two children (who eventually received orphan relative status). All of a sudden, the young man found himself in a position where he had a lot of responsibilities, quite unexpectedly and at an early age. This perhaps precipitated the man's early marriage to have someone to assist with looking after the children (Professional 2).

Specific issues for carers then include:

- Carers may suddenly be notified that close relatives have died/are missing, perhaps under traumatic circumstances and be expected, feel obliged to help the orphan(s) relative
- May re-live some of their own past traumatic experiences as a result of the re-settlement process
- Suddenly need to assist a relative's child/children who might be in a desperate and difficult situation

- Applying for an Orphan Relative Visa may potentially be stressful and frustrating, expensive and time consuming
- Having to care for a relative unexpectedly, someone they may not actually even know
- Potential conflict situation with orphan(s) and or/family members.

Issues specifically for orphan(s)

Box 6 highlights the emotional and psychological complexities involved that impact on the lives of the orphans. Specific issues also include:

- May feel a sense of relief initially that they are safe in Australia, but later trauma may re-surface and come to the forefront
- Might repress and/or not understand their own traumatic experiences and 'act out' in a way carer and others might not understand
- May feel unable to talk about their experiences to others who in turn may not be able to understand their behaviour
- May encounter problems coming to terms with new culture and way of life (see Cultural Issues)
- May experience intergenerational conflict and tensions over questions of their identity and about 'who they are' in Australian society.

Box 6: Emotional distress of orphan(s)

Professional 9

Orphans often come from war torn and conflict areas [with] a history of torture and trauma … and there are issues of adjustment. It is common for the child to feel sad [and lack] a sense of safety once they arrive, [as] they don't feel that they are part of the family they have entered. Often carers have their own child and [orphan(s)] can feel like 'add-on's'. This can create family conflict.

Professional 11

[Re-settlement] puts young people emotionally in pause mode in terms of settlement outcomes. [They] move on and ticking off [and] learning new things; a pausing effect means emotionally there is not necessarily a drive to look for activities that would normally help people integrate and find what they would like to do within the new environment. [For the orphans] feelings of being a burden and being rejected can weigh heavily [on them] and there are elements of shame there as well. It is difficult to address trauma that might have happened from home and it produces young people not being good self-advocates as well.

Professional 8

Some children get depressed and cry all the time, and some act out and get angry at the carer, kids that are reacting to something that they have seen or experienced.

Professional 10

Racism can impact [on] the community or the family. People are stressed, less trusting of services and disengaging. For example, the Afghani/Iraqi community are concerned that every five minutes someone is questioning whether they are a security threat. [It's like the] daily stressors [of] dripping tap Chinese water torture [and] the wearing nature of it, where it's not only a roadblock, but also the fact that there is something every day that builds up stress. A lot of the young guys [also] have a huge sense of family responsibility and they often support family in other countries, which can be a [big] financial issue for them.

Cultural issues

> People from rural Ethiopia will tell this boy before he leaves for Australia that he will go 'to paradise', so his expectations are very high … The orphan might come back from school and wants brand new (designer shoes) which the mother would never buy for her own children, but the orphan boy insists, thinking that the government would pay for it and can't understand that this is not the way it works here. So orphans might end up being very demanding, wanting more and more so that all family members get concerned. Then they don't know what to do anymore (Professional 7).

Most informants thought that culture is an important issue that affects the re-settlement experience of the orphan(s) as well as the living situation for the carer. While some participants thought that culture can either have a positive or negative influence on peoples' experiences, many thought that the arrival of an orphan(s) may lead to many misunderstandings, frustration and additional stresses for all concerned. As Box 7 demonstrates, they saw culture as complex and that even a national culture may include internal variety and conflict.

Box 7: Cultural complexities

Culture Shock

There may also be a 'culture clash' between everyone concerned. This will especially apply until the orphan knows the language, the system and the way everything works in their new surroundings. The orphan might initially be confused and misunderstand many things (Professional 10).

Cultural Positives and Negatives

Cultural traditions can be both positive and negative. The positives are that [orphan(s)] may actually have multiple relatives and guardians, which means that a child has a wider variety of people in their lives. Also, the children often feel that they have been given an opportunity by coming to Australia and are therefore ambitious and want to achieve educationally. The negatives [include] that boys [are allowed] to do more, whereas girls are much more restricted. For example, girls often won't go to the language centre campus. They often won't even ask the carers. Girls are often seen as an additional hand for child caring … and stay at home to look after the carer's child, because the carer is absent having to do something. The girls might not like it, but they also know that it is expected of them, whereas the boys don't need to do that (Professional 9).

Cultural Complexities within the same National Culture

Children may also look different to their carers, something which could make them feel strange and alienated. They may think that they don't look like their parents. For example, one of the Vietnamese 'airlift babies' felt that when she grew up she didn't look like her adoptive mother who sent the girl to Collingwood to be with other Vietnamese kids. There, the girl also felt isolated as she didn't speak Vietnamese. In the end, the girl was not at home with people looking Caucasian or Vietnamese people. [While example relates to intercountry adoption] many [similar] identity issues may thus arise in a re-settlement/placement situations (Professional 1).

While both the host family and orphan might be called 'Ethiopian', they might be quite different. If the carer, let's say, comes from Addis Ababa the capital of Ethiopia, a modern city like here in Australia … where everything is updated and the orphan comes from a small town or regional city, the orphan might not know anything and they have very little in common. Kids from the countryside may be considered backward in Addis Ababa and actually be laughed at, because the way they dress and speak. So one can imagine an orphan coming all the way from rural Ethiopia to Melbourne to live … with people who grew up in Addis Ababa. That is a major step! (Professional 14).

Many children are in shock after they arrive and cannot relate to the people they thought would be like the 'Ethiopians', or 'Sudanese' they had known from where they had come from. Host families also treat the children the way they treat their own children and the way they do things in their own home may make it even harder [for the orphan(s)] because every household has their own 'policy' … specific house rules which may not work for people who come from overseas (Professional 7).

The complexities of cultural issues are demonstrated again in general and individual dimensions, affecting both groups:

Issues in general

- Experiencing potential culture clash
- Misunderstanding/misinterpreting actions and behaviour
- Potential difficulties/frustrations about not having cultural expectations met.

Issues for carers

- Difficulties in navigating traditional stereo-typical gender roles and modern Australian values and expectations, taught in school/practiced in the community
- Potential difficulties in bridging the cultural divide that may exist between themselves and the orphan(s), despite sharing similar ethnic backgrounds
- Having put much effort into bringing the orphan(s) into Australia, including incurring perhaps substantial expenses, carer(s) may expect gratitude on the part of the orphan(s) and that:
  - female orphan(s) will assist carers in household duties/child rearing
  - male orphan(s) will go to work as soon as possible to support the family
- While some carers might be disappointed when orphan(s) resist playing these traditional roles, other orphan(s) may actually want to conform to them and in turn feel frustrated when carers/members of their family actively discourage them.

Issues for orphan(s)

> Girls more than boys need to be taught how to be responsibly independent and to take responsibility for themselves, to catch a tram from here to there – where it is unlikely that they will be abused, and

> that they can go there by themselves and not need their mother or grandmother in tow to take them. The boys have to learn to look after themselves and also not to throw their weight around with others. For example, one young African man tried to pick up a girl of Turkish background in an inappropriate way and when the girl said 'no' he felt insulted and got angry (Professional 2).

- Experiencing difficulties in understanding, misinterpreting behaviours of:
  - carer and other members of host family
  - other children, teachers in school
  - members of the wider community
- Language difficulties and fitting into the new way of life
- Difficulties in forming a cultural identity and coming to terms with 'who they are'
- Feeling pressured by cultural obligations i.e. to conform and/or do things they really do not wish to do
- Difficulties in knowing how to 'date' appropriately, i.e. how to approach people in a way that is clearly understood and acceptable in the Australian context/community
- Difficulties in connecting with local peer groups as well as those from their own cultural backgrounds
- Experiencing racism in the community
- Feeling frustrated at not having their high expectations met after they have heard so much about how Australia is 'a paradise' and rich country, from other people before they arrive.

Settlement issues

> We don't need to see them everywhere with drugs, being upset or something, we bring them here to have a good life. We don't bring them to Australia just to throw them away like rubbish … kids especially from Africa need help from us because they [are already] divided

> and most of them [had] a very hard life. … They don't have a mum, they don't have a dad and they even haven't got love when they are young, so they really need help as they don't know who they are and still trying to be someone (Professional 14).

According to all informants, the settlement experience of orphan(s) is complex and difficult for both the carers and orphan(s), as Box 8 illustrates.

Box 8: Example of the complexity of resettlement experience

For Professional 1, the key questions/issues are:

- How well do carers know the orphan(s)?
- How much information was given to the carers to prepare them before the child comes to live with them and to think through the issues and implications for them?
- How well has placement been thought out before the orphan(s) arrive?
- How much support will they get in terms of caring for a child they have never met before?
- How will they get to know that child, build a relationship with them and work through the issues and problems which will undoubtedly arise in the future?
- How much support will there be down the track when things get a bit harder when the kid gets older and an adolescent?
- We don't know anything about the wishes of the carers or orphan(s)

For Professional 12:

At first there could be bewilderment … even at something like transport. I remember working with a young person who went: 'Oh my god, there's cars everywhere!' Some of them said to me: 'At night in my country there's people walking around at night, we know our neighbours.' In Australia it's true, you go to the suburbs come 6 or 7 o'clock there's no one in the streets, they're all in their homes. The way we live our lives in Australia is so different in that sense. Some young people go, 'I don't feel safe going out at night because there's no one in the streets. In my country there's people I know everywhere.' Even a small thing like that can be quite confronting. Other small things could be things we take for granted in Australia, like opening the papers and thinking 'can the newspapers say that about the politicians?' in other countries people get put to death if you say those things about politicians. There's freedom of speech here, you won't get picked up by the police if you say you don't like certain things. Some of those things are very intangible things and giving them and their carer's information so that they know. It's information on one level, it's also a psychological adjustment to a different space we live in. Adjusting the language is an example, families study English abroad but once they come they are sometimes unable to understand people here because they speak 'funny'. You can have the knowledge but whether you successfully use that knowledge in everyday practice is another thing, it takes time to get used to.

Issues in general include:

- Potential difficulties in establishing trusting relationships
- Unrealistic expectations
- Insufficient support
- Inadequate preparation for the settlement experience.

Issues for carers

> For instance, the young carer is say 19 years old and the orphan coming in is 14 or 15, there can be difficulties and issues in the young boy not understanding this relationship and what it actually entails, i.e. one is responsible for the other. He may therefore not be accepting the young carer's authority at all, nor show the necessary respect required, perhaps thinking that 'he can't tell me what to do, tell me that I should go to school, or what I should eat, wear or behave', etc. The orphan may also have no understanding of the cost involved in running a household, how expensive things are and the fact that the young carer may be struggling to make ends meet (Professional 2).

- Having to deal with orphans' unrealistic expectations and demands
- Being inexperienced in dealing with complex re-settlement issues
- Lacking adequate community support to assist with re-settlement process
- Being insufficiently prepared for the difficulties which may occur
- Having their expectations unfulfilled/frustrated as orphan(s) may be unwilling to cooperate or disagree with what is expected
- Lacking clarity about their legal rights, responsibilities and obligations

Issues for orphans

> Gender issues become [one of] the biggest issues for girls [and] the expectations of girls are very different [to those of boys]. In terms of education … the expectation is that the girl finishes [school] soon, whereas it is expected that the boy does something after school. That again reinforces that boys are going to go out there into the wider community and the girls are going to stay [at] home. [While boys] can go and live with their friends, girls [have to] live in the family home and due to a lack of space, girls may be getting married quicker so that they can move out. [In fact] it seems that the girls on the 117 visa are getting married quite young [compared to] other girls on a different visa (Professional 9).

- Unrealistic expectations of carer/host family and the wider community
- Inadequate preparation for the re-settlement experience and the new situations in host family, school, wider community
- Potential difficulties in engaging with carer/host family, peers in school and social networks
- Possible difficulties in understanding Australian legal and other systems and the fact that they now have certain freedoms, rights and obligations
- Insufficient specialised community support and advice
- Possible difficulties with gender/sexual relationships
- Possible contact with the juvenile justice system, after offending behaviour
- Difficulties in entering the Australian school system/job market.

Summary

Based on the interviews conducted with the key professional informants, a number of important issues were identified that impacted on the resettlement process and lives of orphans and their kinship carers. These issues included: having insufficient financial and other resources; inadequate accommodation; emotional/psychological issues; cultural complexities; and resettlement issues.

While insufficient financial and other resources often made it difficult for both orphans and their kinship carers to make ends meet, inadequate accommodation further exacerbated difficulties. Past emotional and psychological trauma sometimes negatively affected settlement and some experiences in the new surroundings could increase stress and anxiety. Culture was seen as a complex and important issue which could affect re-settlement either positively or negatively. For many orphans, the new cultural settings presented challenges, including racism in some cases and difficulties in fitting into a new society/way of life. These challenges could also involve their carers as both groups at times struggled to comprehend each others' experiences.

The overall resettlement experience thus depended on many factors, including the adequacy of and knowledge about support and resources, the kind of expectations on both sides, and the sufficiency of individual coping mechanisms. In addition some carers and orphans were uncertain about their rights and obligations under Australian law.

4.2 The needs of carers and orphans

Needs discussed in this section relate to the issues identified in the previous section. The aim is to further accentuate and extend these insights into the experiences of both the carers and the orphans. Needs thus expressed by the informants, underscore what people are lacking and what is required for both groups to have better lives. As shown in Box 9, needs identified include: financial/resources, accommodation/housing, emotional/psychological, cultural and needs related to the resettlement process.

Box 9: Needs identified

- Financial/Resources
- Accommodation
- Emotional/Psychological
- Culture
- Resettlement

Financial/resource needs

> The arrival of an additional child or children might increase the insufficient financial resources for the whole family, especially if there is no discrimination towards the biological children and other family members at the expense of the new child. This then may depress the whole living standard of the family, affecting the availability of resources to meet basic needs such as food, clothing, etc. If the child/young person goes to school, there will be additional needs/expectations e.g. having an iPad and other devices that are seen as requirements by the children/school, putting extra pressures on the family (Professional 1).

Most informants suggested that both carers and orphan(s) lack sufficient financial resources after the arrival of the orphan(s). This then impacts on the lives of both groups in various ways. By extension, the lack of necessary resources may endanger the re-settlement process of the orphan(s).

In general, it was found that there are insufficient financial resources to cover:

- Accommodation/housing related expenditures
- Day-to-day living expenses
- Employment/educational expenses
- Health/well-being related costs
- Social/recreational outlays.

Specifically for carers/host family

Box 10 shows some examples of the needs of some of the carers and illustrates financial hardships experienced when bringing up additional children. It further demonstrates how carers sometimes get into debt trying to bring relative children into the country and look after them. In this context, research identified funding as inadequate to meet the various needs of the carers, other family members and those of the orphan(s). This then meant the inability to afford:

- Housing, utilities and other bills

- Alternative accommodation if current residence is overcrowded
- Food, groceries, clothing
- Children's/young peoples' school expenses, including excursions
- Added health care costs such as co-payments, dental care, specialised health and mental health care costs associated with possible chronic and/or past disabilities and trauma experienced by orphan(s)
- Legal advice/representation
- Items that are seen as necessary by peer groups/school and/or the community, including laptops/computers, internet access, mobile phone/iPods, 'designer' clothes and shoes, etc.

Box 10: Examples of financial needs of carers

General example:

Bringing up children is expensive and an extra child adds to the burden. The way a family can cope often depends on what kinds of Centrelink benefits can be made available, unless the family is relatively financially secure. A family without adequate financial resources cannot provide the children with the specialist support they need, i.e. emotional/psychological care since this is not part of the public system. If the educational needs of an orphan are not met and problems are not remedied there is a risk of alienation/disaffection. Lack of money for school excursions, may mean for example that the child may be treated differently to the others. In a family with other children, inadequate financial resources might mean that preferential treatment goes to the natural children (in some circumstances new child might end up as servant/maid in the family (Professional 1).

Being indebted:

To get people here everybody borrowed everything from everybody and there are all sorts of debts I don't know how they pay them back … and I don't know whether it works or doesn't but they are ok people that got not much money but magically the money that is needed comes, so somewhere along the lines, somebody stood in for them and got money, so they are usually people who are on income support and payments themselves, they often got their own children that they are already providing for, often nobody is working or got some sort of disability (Professional 2).

[Carers] borrow money to cope [and] it's [then] the added burden of returning that money also … When the Centrelink money comes through it goes back to repaying that debt. For example If I am getting a $100 from Centrelink and $50 goes towards repaying then I'm only living on $50. It's a challenge (Professional 4).

For the orphans

> Orphan children would need a carer who understands what they are going through. A school setting that knows their history and would be able to support them. They would need access to funds for activities, they don't have Centrelink support for the first couple of years and if carers don't know about entitlements then they won't be able to apply to get them (Professional 13).

While the orphans are supported by their carers, financial resources are often insufficient. There is also a need for orphans to have money of their own. Informants thus suggest that there is no independent source of income i.e. youth allowance, to:

- Buy personal things which carer may not be able to afford or considers unnecessary
- Afford school/study related expenses
- Engage in recreational activities carer cannot/doesn't want to pay for
- Pay for leisure activities with friends
- Enjoy extracurricular activities.

Accommodation

> Children in an Australian family should ideally have their own bedroom… rather than having them sharing with one of the other children in the house. This would especially apply in this situation … [when] the child/young person is a total stranger. This then comes back to financial issues since there is no financial support and the family would need to be fairly wealthy to have a spare room for the additional child. But if there is no extra room the child just has to 'bunk in' and in a different culture that might be expected, although in Australia that will be a problem (Professional 1).

For most participants, the need for appropriate and affordable housing is central to the successful re-settlement of the orphans, affecting not only their lives but also those of their carers and host families, as Box 11 demonstrates.

Box 11: Example of accommodation needs

Need for Separate Rooms

[Accommodation needs] are not just a problem in terms of physical amenities but also in terms of the other children and how they feel about having another child coming into their space and family. For example, if they are forced to share [we don't know] what might happen in the bedroom [like] bullying, racist comments, needling or whatever. While the whole family should have adequate room if [I were] assessing [the situation] I wouldn't want to rule out anyone on that basis – but we are talking ideals now (Professional 1).

Bigger Families and Potential Dislocation

There is a need for appropriate housing for big families. Often you see family dislocation, [because a] family may have a two bedroom apartment and then another two kids come to live with them. [But] in order for the family to get appropriate accommodation, they have to shift out and they often don't want to because that is where they have their community links. Families [may therefore] prefer to have inappropriate housing [rather] than [having] to move away from their community links (Professional 9).

Bigger Families and Rental Market

It's a tenuous position to be a renter with a big family and expensive to get a big property. [People] can also be discriminated against if they have a large family and there can be issues of overcrowding. It's amazing how they make good use of such small spaces because they are not unaccustomed to it. It also increases the tendency to compare themselves to other people who have bigger properties where each child may have a room for themselves (Professional 13).

General accommodation needs thus included:

- Access to affordable alternative housing
- Adequate living space
- Sufficient private and personal space
- Appropriate/sufficient amenities.

Carers' specific needs

> The sponsor family itself is living in very cramped conditions. [Sometimes] there are large families living in 2 or 3 bedroom units and [then]

> there's an additional person in that place. Often things are going to happen even when they [the orphans] belong to the same family, if they live in such close proximity and if the relationship breaks down. If it gets to a point where you can't retrieve the relationship, the new member becomes homeless because they are the newest [member] in the family (Professional 4).

Carers require sufficient room/space:

- To manage household effectively
- To feel comfortable and at home
- To have privacy and personal respite
- For recreational activities/hobbies at home
- For intimacy with others, including their spouse, existing family/ biological children
- To meet other people, family and friends.

Orphan(s) specific needs

Orphans need sufficient space/room to be able:

- To be independent
- To develop a sense of belonging
- To work/study
- To be alone, by themselves/independent
- To meet people, develop friendships
- To have privacy, feel comfortable and safe.

Emotional/psychological needs

Many key informants stated that the emotional and psychological needs of both the carers and orphans are high and adequate support needs to be provided and considered to make the settlement process successful. While some of the needs of both groups overlap, there are also marked differences as shown in Box 12 below.

General needs

In general terms, both groups need to:

- Feel understood, valued, appreciated
- Feel and be safe
- Have their needs met
- Come to terms with past and present experiences, potential conflict
- Have sufficient personal and community support
- Overcome past and present traumatic experiences.

Box 12: Examples of emotional/psychological support needs

Carers Support Needs

Emotional and psychological issues are enormous problems among carers. A lot of them are grandparents who are older, tired with more health problems and often less money. Parenting when one is older is more challenging, especially with kids who are troubled. This can lead to high levels of stress, anxiety, conflict in the family, mental health issues and even depression. Older host parents might also have trouble holding it all together, have their own family to deal with, perhaps still working, plus having to build a relationship with a new child who is acting out and they don't understand very well. That is why carers need dedicated specialist support services, with well trained workers that understand the specific issues involved. Carers also need professional and personal supports, and being able to talk to other people who have either a professional or personal understanding about the issues they are facing. A lot of carers say that they need respite either through their friends or their networks (Professional 1).

Orphan(s) Support Needs

There is a need to have an appropriate transition period during which children's educational, health, emotional needs are met and the trauma they have experienced is addressed. The emotional needs of these children are really high. Sometimes the carers aren't in-tune to what those are. These issues can [resurface] and so it's important for the child to have support, perhaps for someone to check in with them from time to time and hear their views and voice. This process is critical when working with children that have not had a pre and post placement assessment (Professional 3).

Carer needs

> Carers would also need access to supports just like the children ... but there are not very many support [programmes] in the grief and loss area. [Some organisations] do settlement support [such as] housing, etc. but they [often] don't do counselling and cannot access a psychologist to work on attachment issues (Professional 8).

Carers specifically need:

- Good personal, social/community support
- Professional advice/support to assist with resettlement
- Immigration advice
- Initial settlement training, parental seminars
- Information about community services availability and access
- Provision of child rights based information
- Legal support/guidance on orphan children/young people and on relevant norms/requirements of Australian law
- Additional financial support and advice
- Opportunities for respite/recuperation
- Assistance with locating alternative housing if accommodation is overcrowded.

Orphans' needs

> Orphan children and young people need a lot of support ... counselling and settlement programs (Professional 8).

Orphans specifically need:

- An understanding and supportive host family/carer and community

- To have specialised professional/community support when and if required
- To have their basic and higher needs fully met
- To feel safe and secure in their new home and community
- To have independent spaces and privacy
- To deal with emotional/psychological issues/stress arising from their past experience and their new environment
- To come to terms with unrealistic expectations, new culture and surroundings, and to develop a new identity
- To have the ability to move on and feel they have a future
- To have meaningful social/cultural engagements
- To have a supportive and understanding school and community environment
- To understand the law e.g. their rights and obligations in Australia.

Cultural needs

> There [sometimes] is a very Caucasian middle class bias in terms of who gets approved as an adoptive parent who is the one with a spare bedroom and all that, with a reasonable income who can then give the kids the extra things that they might need. But it actually might be more important for that child to go into a family who either doesn't have much or really wants to embrace the kids, feeling somewhat attuned [to the culture], lets say a Somali family who hasn't been here that long and hasn't got much but they understand very well what is happening at home [overseas] and they just want to pull that child in and they might bunk in with eight kids but that might work out (Professional 1).

Many of the participants, both carers and orphans, have cultural needs which all stakeholders involved need to take into consideration. However, these needs are complex in that individuals 1) have cultural needs which need to be fulfilled and satisfied and 2) need to be able to do certain things and behave in certain ways. So not only do carers and orphans have real cultural needs such as having a supportive and understanding environment, they have to develop a cultural awareness themselves, as Box 13 illustrates, for example.

Box 13: The need to be culturally aware and educated

Cultural Anecdote

A guy originally born in Eritrea was living in Ethiopia for a long, long time and after all these years he came to visit his family, not closely [related] to him in Eritrea … In Ethiopia, when you shake someone's hand you shake it in a certain way and in Eritrea they don't have anything like this. So this guy [used the Ethiopian handshake] saying hello to three, four people [in this way]. But soon, people got alarmed and called a doctor and [then] they put him into a mental hospital, thinking he was crazy … So culture can be a barrier but you have to try to understand it and in time [and with effort] you will know it (Professional 7).

Cultural Issues and Expectations

Culture is very important and we would want the carer to be well versed about what the implications are of taking in such a child and know what sort of cultural background this child has come from. Carers need some education around cultural issues and the expectations of the child, equally how they would teach the child about the cultural values they have just moved into (Australian culture). For example, if a Vietnamese host family is taking in a Vietnamese child, we can assume some common cultural traits, but there could also be some differences. The Vietnamese carer may be Australian-born and doesn't exactly know what is happening in Vietnam, the circumstances the child has come from, or the experiences the child might have gone through. Perhaps one practices religion or both of them do, but they may differ in terms of what they expect of religious worship. The child might move into a practicing Christian household but isn't a Christian and then are they expected to adopt that? (Professional 1).

General needs

As Box 14 suggests, both groups also need to be able to change and adapt to new situations when required to avoid many of the possible frustrations/potential challenges, in order to make the resettlement process a success.

Box 14: Fluidity of culture and the need to adapt and change

Culture is fluid anyway and not stagnant and needs to be respected to keep its dignity. And because culture is so fluid, it changes over time. Young people adapt and change much more quickly than the adults do. When we are talking about cultural conflict, it's really about inter-generational conflict, interpreting the rules, the dos and the don'ts in the family unit and how things are interpreted differently over time. The longer young people stay and settle the more Western they become. At the same time, the adults become more old fashioned, so to speak, because they are hanging on to what they feel comfortable with, while the young generation is challenging that. I actually think that this is something that also happens in our Anglo Australian families. Each generation has got a new group that challenges society and how we view ourselves. I don't see it as unhealthy; I see it as very healthy. Normalising it rather than dramatizing it is the way to go. The experiences of these families happen in most families and in every single generation. I don't think it is culture so much. What does worry me is the role of religion in society, particularly in this day and age, when there is one religion that's almost ostracized or seen as a negative influence on society. It is not the religion, it's the individuals who practice it and interpret it. I think the more exposure a young person has to social networks, the more opportunities they are given to make up their own minds to form their own worldview (Professional 4).

General needs thus identified include:

- Having a supportive and culturally sensitive environment at home and in the community
- Having cultural needs met and maintain relevant social/community connections
- Being able to:
  - understand and respect cultural differences and commonalities
  - re-evaluate expectations, values and traditions
  - learn/adapt to new behaviour patterns if required.

Carer specific

> Aunty, I am wondering, when the children are doing some [house] duty, their mum is always saying 'thank you' to them, but why [he asks] is the mum saying 'thank you' to her own children? [Because] for the boy, it should always be the woman's children who should say 'thank you' to her, so the boy says 'but look she is a mum she became pregnant nine years ago, she did this and she did that and she deserves more than that so why would she do that?' (Professional 7).

Carers need to specifically be able to:

- Maintain their own cultural traditions, beliefs and existing life style as much as that is possible and appropriate, including their religion, community and social links
- Navigate and understand the orphan(s) values/expectations and facilitate their appropriate adaptation/integration into Australian society
- Receive culturally sensitive community support to assist with problems/challenges, including training and education
- Re-evaluate some of their traditions and values so as not to impose them on the orphan(s).

Orphan specific

> Kids find it hard to understand the Western culture and society and [the constant] need for money. Often the children … cannot identify [real] needs and wants, such as food versus a mobile phone. Some kids find it difficult to distinguish between what is more important and often want mobile phones over food and cannot cost these things. A carer would prioritise food over the phone and this becomes a source of conflict when these kids think they are not being given what they want (Professional 9).

Orphans specifically need:

- A culturally sensitive/supportive home and community to assist with their integration/transition
- Appropriate community advice/support to overcome difficulties
- To be able to:
  - re-evaluate their own expectations, traditions and if required adopt new ways and modes of behaviours
  - cope with the unavoidable misunderstandings and inevitable frustrations
  - develop a positive new cultural and personal identity

- learn to integrate appropriately into Australian society, its language and way of life/traditions

- distance themselves from their own traditions if they choose to.

Resettlement needs

> More often than not a young person arrives, and while they are connected with this family, there is no appropriate work done on the relationship. There is no appropriate induction and settlement for the young person that will facilitate the success of the placement. If things do start to break down and get to a critical point, it may well be irreversible. Whereas if there was an organisation, or somebody, providing support in the early phases the crisis may have been prevented (Professional 9).

Successful resettlement depends on many factors, including adequate preparation, sufficient information, community and personal support, and realistic expectations.

General needs

> One of the things we've advocated for is access to Centrelink payments. They [orphans] shouldn't have to wait for two years; there should be no waiting period. Of course with Centrelink payments comes a health care card (Professional 12).

There are a number of general needs in this area, they include:

- Be clear about legal rights, responsibilities and obligations (see Box 15, for instance)
- Develop and establish trusting relationships in the home and community
- Avoid unrealistic expectations
- Have sufficient support at home and community
- Get prepared for the settlement experience.

Box 15: Confusion and misunderstandings about rights and obligations

Australia is one of the most regulated societies in the world, contrasting with Sudan where, for example, no licences are required for driving. For example, one client thought that their library card was a drivers' licence, and was surprised when he was pulled over by the police for not having a licence. Another client bought L-plates from a supermarket and placed them on their car, believing them to signify their possession of a licence. Some don't know about seat belts, or about not putting 5 children in the back seats and fines were often received due to misunderstanding about things such as driving through City-Link without a pass, or smoking in the car with children in the car, or using mobile phones while driving. Many carers need help with migration and citizenship issues which are important milestones in the settlement. Police interactions are also difficult for some communities (i.e. for the Sudanese community), an issue for which families need assistance, along with alcohol education. Young people may also be self-medicating for depression by using alcohol and need access to mental health support services (Professional 5).

Carers

> The carer has all the responsibility of maintaining them [orphans) as well as assisting them with re-settlement. While some of the support needed can be provided by the carers through daily living, the carer may suddenly be confronted with other difficult issues. The carers may also have other people to look after who may have different views and their own life issues to deal with (Professional 2).

Carers specifically need:

- Sufficient settlement information and preparation before the orphan arrives
- Reasonable expectations of themselves and orphan(s) to prevent unnecessary frustrations and conflicts
- Sufficient preparation for any difficulties and a willingness to seek advice and support
- Sufficient financial support in order to meet the needs of all concerned
- Adequate community support to assist with the complex re-settlement process and challenges.

Orphans

> There are also many welfare issues; often the kids coming on the OR visa have come from a history of torture and trauma. It is hard for the teachers to have a good understanding of what's occurred and they often refer them to welfare agencies that can deal with trauma (Professional 9).

Orphans specifically need:

- Sufficient pre-settlement information/preparation to cope with new situations in host family, school and wider Australian community
- A willingness and ability to receive specialised community support and advice if and when required
- Realistic expectations of themselves, carers, and society
- A willingness and ability to engage with carer/host family, peers in school and social networks
- Appropriate language skills, cultural awareness and behaviour (including knowledge of gender/sexual relationships) to be able to function in the community
- New friendships, social activities and ways of life appropriate to their new circumstances
- An understanding of their rights and obligations at home and within the Australian legal and other systems
- To avoid coming into contact with the juvenile justice system
- To prepare well for entering the Australian school system and job market.

Summary

A number of needs were identified by informants in this section. They included key areas such as a lack of financial and other resources, accommodation/housing needs, emotional/psychological and cultural supports. In addition there are needs specific to the resettlement process.

While both groups need adequate financial and other resources, they also require adequate housing with applicable personal/private spaces where they can live and work in reasonable and comfortable conditions. The emotional and psychological wellbeing of both groups is considered important, with carers and orphans in need of support, understanding and specialised assistance from time to time. Both groups have significant cultural needs which require community and personal understanding, tolerance and sensitivity for them to be met and fulfilled.

Successful resettlement then depends on a number of factors, including adequate preparation for the experience, the provision of sufficient information, adequate community and personal support, understanding of rights and responsibilities, as well as everyone concerned keeping their expectations realistic.

4.3 The support carers and orphans require

> At an appropriate point in time, somebody (a service) needs to make contact with the family and let them know what support is available. Depending on the complexity [and] other background issues, sometimes a support worker in a case management type model can be entirely effective and support someone relatively quickly, and in other situations the issues are really complicated and they need someone with a high degree of skill … to work long-term with the family. Good case management and the capacity to link in with good mental health services is what it comes down to and not mandatory but a resource that is available. A good initial assessment must be done in order for it to work; there must be some sort of screening during the first contact. There are families that are highly resilient but there must be a phase for asking [what they need] in a timely way (Professional 10).

Almost all informants agreed that both carers and orphans need to be assisted in the re-settlement process when and if they require it. For many participants, this also entails some sort of an assessment of the family's/orphans' needs and situation (see Section 4.4 for details). Assistance provided is largely intended to prevent the breakdown of the placement. One example of factors contributing to such a breakdown is shown in Box 16 below.

Box 16: Professional 15's factors of potential placement breakdown

Placement breakdown due to:

- A lack of space, overcrowding in the home
- An additional financial burden on the carer
- The impact on the carer's own relationship with their partner
- A negative impact on carer's own situation and ability to meet their needs
- An increased potential for the carer's own relationship to breakdown
- The carer's partner telling them that they can't deal with the extra pressures associated with the child/young person. Partner might demand that the orphan either has to leave immediately or that they have to go elsewhere once they turn 16 (while the orphan/teenager is not ready to leave)
- A negative impact on the care of carer's biological children
- An increased emotional distress in the host family about new allegiances among family members and how carer will prioritise commitment and relationship between orphan and their own children
- An inability of either the carer or the orphan to come to terms with settlement needs
- The negative impact on carer's employment.

In general

> Carers and kids should have access to support services to assist in the integration settlement/process to ensure that things will work out. E.g. if there would be family conflict the young person is already booked with a service, [which] can assist with locating accommodation or there could be severe health issues with the kids where the service could help and assist with getting access to other services. Therefore every family/host should have a service automatically allocated to them at the point of arrival of the young person. It may help if this service could be mandatory (Professional 6).

As Box 17 shows, a number of general support services were suggested by the key informants. These range from the general provision of information and greater financial assistance to offering support and case management services.

Box 17: Selected general support service suggestions

Professional 1

The ideal support system for carers would be:

- The augmentation (increase of service provision) of carers similar to that provided under [local/national] kinship care arrangements, with services like those of Ozchild and Anglicare linked in
- Making additional ad-hoc funding available for a certain number of families for this specialised area, on the child's arrival
- The provision of a case manager, with specialist training in cross-cultural issues, so that the case could be shared across a service team
- The case manager should be well linked to relevant services.

Professional 7

Supports needed to enable the host family to care for the orphan:

- Services should be culturally appropriate and sensitive
- Information to be given about available services as carers may not know the system, their entitlements but also the roles of different organisations, e.g. Centrelink, Medicare, DHS and so on
- Information about the role of professionals
- Information about the carers' responsibilities
- Before carers apply for the child's visa, they should be provided with relevant information so that carers have some understanding about what is involved
- After arrival orphans and carers need information about all aspects of settlement, including legal aspects, rights and responsibilities.

Professional 5

Services needed include:

- A caseworker to be involved with the family for a few years and available until the child is 18, someone who knows the family and can pick up on issues as they arise and link the family in with appropriate services
- Counselling, more of a 'spotting exercise', especially if someone has had depression or post-traumatic stress
- Greater financial support and a higher level of income from Centrelink
- Appropriate accommodation/housing adequate to family needs
- In terms of counselling, assistance with communication between school and home which often does not currently happen/work well. Teachers want to do the best they can for everyone, but are often unaware of what is occurring at home, e.g. 7 people living in the home, thus it would be unfair to punish a child for not completing homework or 'treating them like they are dumb'.

For carers

Specific support services suggested for carers include:

- Settlement support for the new arrival(s) that is at least equivalent to other programmes, e.g. international adoption, domestic kinship or foster care resettlement
- Culturally sensitive and appropriate case management/community services (immediately after arrival) that are not tied to government (preferably from the NGO sector) to identify/assess the needs of carer/host family and those of orphan children/young people in order to assist and support them
- Possible specific support requirements include:

  - initial provision of information/advice about settlement experience
  - financial assistance
  - access to community resources and services
  - location of alternative housing if required
  - emotional and psychological support to assist in coping with the new situation
  - relevant legal advice, e.g. what behaviour, actions are appropriate under Australian law.

For orphans

Box 18 shows a selection of support services suggested by the informants to improve the orphans' well-being, for them to succeed and become productive members of society.

Box 18: Selected support service suggestions for orphans

If you put the correct intervention in place early on, in a timely manner, in our experience at least 80% of orphans have succeeded. They have completed their [educational] courses, are employed in meaningful jobs and have become productive members of society and have a lot to give (Professional 8).

We don't need to see them everywhere with drugs, being upset or something, we bring them here to have a good life. We don't bring them to Australia just to throw them away like rubbish … kids especially from Africa need help from us because they [are already] already divided and most of them [had] a very hard life … They don't have a mum, they don't have a dad and they even haven't got love when they are young, so they really need help as they don't know who they are and still trying to be someone (Professional 14).

I think [we need] something similar to settlement services … Somebody who is geared towards young people and their mental health. But that role is actually quite complex, because your primary client is that young person and that young person is more vulnerable because they are new. But your other role is in supporting that family and you can't be policing. You need to be working in partnership with the family. But the partnership also has to be that the parents understand that there are certain obligations that the state needs you to meet and if these obligations are not met then these are the consequences and those consequences need to be significant enough for them to carry out that responsibility. So that not everybody brings another child here, or every child that comes into the country is given that opportunity (Professional 4).

To assist the orphans to succeed, specific support requirements include:

- Strong peer support networks
- Loving, understanding/flexible and supportive family environment
- English language classes/educational support
- Counselling for past traumatic events and grief and loss issues
- Culturally appropriate and sensitive teenage advice/support in relation to gender, sexuality and legal/family law issues
- Health screening on arrival
- Good community and peer support
- Access to child protection and other relevant services when needed/appropriate
- Appropriate community service referrals/linkages.

Summary

This section looked at the support needs of the carers and orphans, where almost all key informants argued that both groups need support to make the re-settlement process of the orphans successful. A range of supports were suggested including service linkages, the general provision of information, greater financial assistance, general and specialised support, including case management services.

For many participants, support also needs to include some assessment of the family's/orphans' needs and situation (see Section 4.4 for details). Assistance provided should at least be equivalent to other programmes, e.g. international adoption/resettlement programmes. The support envisaged was considered essential to preventing the breakdown of the placement.

Overall, there was a strong sense that the support should be 'offered' rather than be compulsory. Assistance should therefore be provided in a spirit of cooperation to build trust with potentially vulnerable people and communities and that it be provided by experienced community based organisations in a culturally sensitive manner. The focus was thus on offering information, assistance and support on a voluntary rather than mandatory basis.

4.4 System improvements

> When you are bringing an orphan over here you need something like a social worker or someone to educate both of them [carer and orphan] and assist and help them with the re-settlement … and it would be good to develop a course or training for the [host] family and orphan (Professional 14).

While in the previous main sections informants largely agreed/added to the information other participants provided (e.g. under Sections 4.1 – 4.3), there were some differences of opinion and even polarised views among the informants about how to improve the system. The two main perspectives are presented in Tables 2–4, broadly presenting the varying views of the research participants on assessments, visa issues and supports required. Given the vulnerable state of children and risks associated with their placement, there was also certain ambivalence in the informants' responses about the best course of action, before and after the orphans come to Australia. The various options are presented within the main perspectives outlined below and amalgamated in Table 1.

Table 1: Phases of involvement and support process

Phase 1: Home visit/ Information gathering	1. Visiting and talking to carers/host families and orphans about their situation, will give experienced workers a good idea of the presenting circumstances and what may be needed 2. Establish trust and rapport with carers and orphans 3. The focus here is on offering assistance/support rather than on 'checking up' on people 4. Follow-up support, i.e. case management can be offered/be recommended to family
Phase 2: Monitoring	1. Monitor carer/orphan situation, if concern has been noted/ identified 2. 'Informal' relationship between worker and family may need to change and carer/orphans be advised
Phase 3: Intervention	1. If reason for concern arises, organise intervention to ensure orphan is safe and their needs are met 2. Mandatory involvement of services may need to occur 3. Liaison with key players to ensure consistency and transparency.

Assessments

> … Mandatory assessments of carers' suitability [should not be considered and] be taken out. My concern is for some of the really worthy carers I have worked with, that someone might come to their home and say 'you're poor, your resources are already stretched' … or if they assess that person, a lot of those carers might have mental health issues themselves … and then they will be deemed ineligible. While I admit that it's not ideal to live with someone who is poor and has a mental health problem, I don't think it's fair to deny them the visa on that basis; I don't think the child's better off in their country of origin. I think it should be about treating those things rather than letting those things exclude them (Professional 5).

While some informants thought that a formal mandatory assessment is crucial for the resettlement process to succeed, many others formulated a different version of 'assessing' carer/orphans' situations and their needs and how then to progressively monitor and intervene if need be (see Table 1). The emphasis was on a supportive and preventative approach rather than 'checking up on them' and a heavy-handed assessment focussed process (see also Box 19 about how the two approaches articulated by the informants differ).

Table 2 shows the key informants' main perspectives in relation to assessment. While the different positions appear weighted towards a voluntary assessment process, participants share a common concern for the welfare of the orphans and the risks resettlement can pose. For this reason, they found it difficult to be certain about prescribing the best course of action in relation to pre and post-assessments.

Table 2: Participants' views on assessments

Perspectives	Assessments
Dominant view	• Voluntary • Ideally, carer and orphan consultations before placement • Informal and culturally sensitive • Appropriate community agency visit after arrival • To gauge needs/what might be required • Safety/protective concerns to be noted and then monitored/acted upon • Concerns about traditional 'middle-class' bias in assessments used to screen out poorer carers and what could be considered 'inappropriate carers/situations'
Minority view	• Mandatory • To check on carer's suitability and their circumstances • Pre and post-arrival assessments of carer and orphan • Mandatory ongoing checking/monitoring family
Combination view	• A Mandatory/voluntary mix that combines other views • voluntary mix that combines other views • Includes both dominant and minority features.

Suggested process for both carers and orphans

While there was some ambivalence in the informants' responses, on balance their views suggest that:

- Ideally there should be some initial consultation offered to potential carers before the orphans' arrival to see if they have all the relevant information and are ready to receive the orphan

- Attempt, if possible/appropriate, to elicit the voices and wishes of orphans before arrival

- After the arrival of the orphan, a post-placement visit to the carer/host family be required by an experienced and appropriate community based agency, rather than a government organisation. This is to:

  - provide information to both carers and orphans about available services/resources

  - answer questions about settlement processes

  - establish trust and respect with family and gauge carer/orphan situation

  - offer support/assistance

  - establish needs/issues if relevant

  - note issues of concerns which may need follow-up

  - organise further support/case management if required/is accepted

  - develop initial care plan with carer/orphans if appropriate.

Box 19: Differing views on assessments

Appropriate monitoring versus 'assessment'

I don't know [about assessments]. I think one of the difficulties with these communities, especially the ones that put their hands up to sponsor, [is that] they see it as being judged by the dominant community. If I was a mother of 4 young children and put my hand up to bring my niece or nephew over and if you came to my house, I'd actually be offended. I already have 4 children of my own and what makes this other child more important than mine? They're offering to help this child and we run the risk of offending communities and need to be careful. Monitoring afterwards is different and they need to be told that they are going to be monitored. There are certain responsibilities that they have to the state and the child and regardless of the circumstances the child's mental health and wellbeing comes first. But I think an 'assessment' may offend some communities. I'd be very worried about that. When I think assessment I think of couples that have been told that they are too old to adopt. I think an assessment, particularly of the Horn of Africa communities that thrive on the family unit and the sharing and the love they have for each other, [would be counterproductive]. You know that old saying 'it takes a village to bring up a child' is so true in these groups you can actually see here in Australia. If there is a woman who is unwell and she is a single mother with little children, she just has to ask the community and the children are looked after while she's in hospital and doesn't matter how many days she spends there. The children are safe because of the way they live and share their responsibilities. I'm torn between the two. I can see the need for an assessment but I also think it can be offensive to some groups (Professional 4).

Assessments would be a waste of money and [I] cannot see the purpose behind it. In my experience, no child has ever said they wished they didn't come here. [I] would rather put the money used in an assessment towards an education program here. [If a 'proper'] assessment of the family for suitability, safe environment and resources be done, it would [likely] mean denying them the visa because most of them would not meet the criteria to bring them out. Poor people are usually bringing them out. Denying them a visa would mean trapping orphans in poverty in another country. A majority of [orphans] with the right support are ok and productive (Professional 8).

Pre-assessment of the carers is critical, both there and here. Also, post assessment – it would be ideal if placement was treated like an adoption placement. While it is uncertain that this thoroughness would be likely to occur, a bare minimum – assessment (looking at the main issues/impact on the care of the child), child protection checks, police checks (of carer), should be carried out (Professional 3).

Visa issues

> If the system was such that you could provide [the necessary evidence] more easily, evidence that was acceptable … that you have no family members, [neither] father or mother. At the moment if you come from say Central Africa you don't know where your mother is, [parents] have gone, they are not there, there is no certificate to say what hap-

> pened to them, [may be] the father ran away and took another woman, or parents tried to get away and got killed … how can you prove that they are killed, or people killed in wars, [by definition] refugee situations are such that there are no death certificates issued by doctors on such and such a date (Professional 2).

Most of the participants felt that the Orphan Relative Visa category was an important and significant avenue for giving some of the most vulnerable children and young people better life chances and opportunities. As shown in Table 3, the majority of informants suggested that the first priority is to allow the orphans into the country and then support them and their carers/host families to make the resettlement process successful (see also Table 4). Thus the granting of the visa should not be tied to an assessment of a carer's suitability.

Table 3: Participants' views on visa issues

Perspectives	Visa issues
Majority view	• Granting of visa not tied to assessment of carer's suitability • Visa to be granted even if carer was found unsuitable, in which case alternative placement to be found • Concern that suitability assessments could be used by policy makers to limit number of visas/orphan intake
Minority view	• Tied to assessment of carer's suitability • If carer is not deemed 'suitable' no visa should be granted to orphan • Mandatory child protection checks • Orphan should be 'tracked' and followed up once in the country

Key informants' comments on the visa process thus include:

- The existence of the visa category was welcomed
- Increase, rather than decrease, the number of visas issued per year to meet growing demand/need of orphans around the world
- Improve and speed up the visa process
- Make visa requirements for documentation less onerous, especially in situations/countries where documents are difficult to obtain

- Consider a culturally appropriate and sensitive placement process, either before or after arrival to gauge/ascertain the needs/wishes of both carers and orphan children/young people (post-placement visit)
- Allocate a free non-government community-based case management/re-settlement service to support new arrivals and their host carer/family (as shown in the next section)
- Coordinate the provision of services across the relevant sectors.

Supports required

> While formal assessments give a family a framework to work with when the kids arrive, the family model of sitting with everyone and talking about needs has western connotations and may not work with this group. Most likely a carer would prefer to talk about what her issues are without the child being present and vice versa. After the initial chat with the family, the worker would [possibly] stay on the case and co-ordinate and perhaps refer to a multi-disciplinary team which would support the family (Professional 8).

While not all respondents agreed that support should be voluntary (see Table 4), all informants suggested that it is important and necessary and should be offered to all carers and orphans involved. Many comments here re-iterate informants' views on the types of support needed, as already shown in Section 2.3 and demonstrated in Box 20 on models of support, and in Box 21 on appropriate work practices. There were again a variety of views which, on balance, suggest a mandatory initial post-placement visit by a non-government organisation. The level of support should then be at the discretion of the carer/orphans if there are no protective or other concerns.

Table 4: Participants' views on supports required

Perspectives	Supports required
Majority view	• Voluntary • Ideally, information to be provided to carer/orphan before placement • To assist/support • On-going case management offered if needed • Support provided by appropriate community based organisation • Concerns monitored and acted upon
Minority view	• Mandatory/some mandatory • Child protection and other government agency involvement
Alternative combination	• Some mandatory/voluntary that combine other views.

Supports suggested for both groups

> You don't have to be Ethiopian to work with Ethiopians but you have to know the culture [and should] have read about it to understand … and respect people (Professional 7).

Box 20 shows a selection of support models put forward by informants. These largely re-iterate previous articulations in relation to the provision of support services and how they should be conducted.

In general terms, it was therefore suggested that:

- Both carers/host family and orphans be supported through the placement, before and after arrival

- A suitably experienced community-based organisation (rather than a government agency) be available to:
  - initially visit the family and offer support in an appropriate way
  - clearly establish needs and issues if required/appropriate
  - provide on-going support in a culturally sensitive and appropriate way on a voluntary basis (see Box 21, for instance) if there are no protective concerns
  - provide/facilitate access to required services
  - consider where appropriate, a mentoring role by suitably qualified

volunteers

- offer relevant information and training both before and after settlement
- provide specific information to potential carers i.e. information packs/CDs.

Box 20: Selected models of support

What is lacking at the moment is:

- The whole family must be supported and some likely scenarios must be talked through when the application is submitted or approved and before the child arrives
- An information pack (maybe a CD) in different languages, giving information on what to expect etc. and perhaps someone watching it with the family (perhaps a worker from a community based agency to explain/answer questions)
- A settlement agency that is responsible for co-ordinating the supports after orphan arrival and assisting them to make sure they get the services/supports required
- A caseworker to be available and meet them perhaps initially once a week just to see how everything was going
- For the family to be open and trusting, they have to see the agency as supportive and it cannot be the DIBP or a government agency
- Relevant training/provision of information so that carer/orphans will be aware of the issues/needs so they can tap into resources before a crisis might emerge
- As there may be tensions/difficulties after arrival, the carer and orphans may benefit from a series of counselling sessions after initial settlement (Professional 8).

Some children may not need as much support as others, each case is different. It is important to note that although initially a family may not need support, they may need it later down the track. There is a need for a basic framework or tool in how to work with OR visa cases. A simplistic form might involve the child being assessed in the first two weeks of their arrival. Then an assessment is completed by a worker making recommendations for a care plan in terms of what the child's needs are and how they would be met. This care plan would then be reviewed every 3–9 months and within that time, the worker can link the carers and children/young people in with their community. It would be best practice if the assessor who conducted the assessment and built rapport with the carers and young people, will also work with them later. They can then identify what extra support is needed, how it can be accessed, make the necessary referrals and also do some of the supportive work with the family. Based on experience, best practice would be to offer this support in the initial 6 months of the child's arrival as it is known that placements are likely to break down in the first 6–12 months. However, if the family feel supported in this initial period then there is a greater chance that the child's placement will succeed (Professional 3).

Some of the views articulated above are illustrated in a selected range of relevant work practices shown in Box 21. Views here again highlight the need to work in a culturally sensitive and appropriate manner.

Box 21: Selected work practices

Working in a Culturally Appropriate/Sensitive Way

One example of how things can go wrong is when I started to work at my current workplace. Then I became aware of an old Ethiopian man in his 70s. The man had been matched with a very young social worker in her 20s, who wore a very short dress. The worker met the old man in the waiting room, shook the old man's hand and ask him to be seated. Then she asked him what the problem was 'in front of everybody'. So the man was shocked and embarrassed and 'didn't like it this way and straight away he opened the door and called out for me'. When the other worker arrived and asked 'what happened?' he said 'look my daughter how do you want me to tell my problem to a grandchild? Her age is like my grandchild, how can I talk to her?' After this incidence, staff at the centre met to discuss this issue and people from different backgrounds all agreed that in their home countries, the elderly were more respected and could relate to the old man's feelings. They then supported [the necessity to work culturally appropriately]. Some of them said we came from Italy we respect our elderly, some of them said they came from Germany there is a respect for our older community, some of them said they came somewhere [else] and all of us we meet [and agreed] that [the] aged are more respected in our own countries. Staff then engaged in cross-cultural discussions about working with this kind of situation appropriately, trying to understand different cultural settings of staff and that of the patient (Professional 7).

Potential Positive Role of Mentoring

There is also a resistance of people seeking official (professional) help and a mentor (unofficial) could provide informal support as part of the community. While this is a good idea, issues may also arise with unofficial workers/mentors/volunteers who are not trained. They would need to have training in terms of what is required in a community mentoring best practice model (like in the community housing sector, for example). Mentoring should not be done by a so-called 'good hearted volunteer persons' without training. While providing financial assistance is good, it needs to come with the knowledge of where to get services and how to access them. It would be good for carers to have some of this knowledge and be and willing to accept that (Professional 2).

Summary

In this section, informants expressed some differences of opinion and exhibited polarised views about how to improve the system. Broadly speaking, these views related largely to issues of assessments, visa issues and supports required. A certain ambivalence was noted in the informants' responses to what might be the best course of action, before and after the orphans come to Australia. This clearly reflected the informants' concern about the vulnerable state of the orphans and the risks and associated issues with their placement. While some informants thought that undertaking a formal mandatory assessment is crucial for the resettlement process to succeed, many others formulated a different version of 'assessing' carers'/orphans' situations and their needs, and how then to progressively monitor and intervene if needed. The majority view emphasised a supportive and subsequently preventative approach rather than a heavy-handed assessment–focussed process.

Most of the participants felt that the Orphan Relative Visa category was an important and significant avenue for the orphans to have better life chances and opportunities. In this context, it was felt that the first priority is to allow the orphans into the country and then support them and their carers/host families to make the resettlement process successful. Thus the granting of the visa should not be tied to an assessment of a carer's suitability and should still be granted even if the carer is found unsuitable.

While not all respondents agreed that support should be voluntary, all agreed that it is necessary and should be offered to the carers and orphans involved. Many comments here re-iterate the informants' earlier views on the types of support needed. On balance, key informants suggested an initial post-placement visit by an experienced NGO. The level of support should then be at the discretion of the carers/orphans if there are no protective or other concerns. The kind of support that should be offered again reflects informants' views that assistance should be provided in a spirit of cooperation to build trust and that an experienced organisation outside the mandatory system would be best suited to deliver this service in a culturally sensitive manner.

5. Conclusion and Recommendations

This study examined the issues, needs, support requirements and future service responses of children and young people who arrive in Australia on Orphan Relative Visas and of their relative/kinship carers. The views of professionals experienced in working with Orphan Relative Visa holders and their kinship carers in Australia were collected through semi-structured interviews and the study has further built on the two previous studies into the Orphan Relative Visa process conducted by ISS (Australia) (Kavanagh, 2011, 2013).

All of these studies confirm that an increasing number of children and young people are arriving in Australia on Orphan Relative Visas, often having come from situations of war, conflict or other traumatic circumstances. While official data show how many children and young people arrive in this way each year, little is known about the post-arrival experiences of the children and their relative carers in Australia. There are no coordinated settlement support services meaning that children and their carers may be connected with a diverse range of services and supports in the community, or in fact not engaged with or able to access any supports. Given that the children and young people often come from situations of conflict and significant trauma, including the loss of parents or other key carers, their individual needs are often significant. Further, their relatives in Australia who take on the caring role are often themselves only recent arrivals, frequently from similar conflict situations, and thus frequently also requiring supports and resources to provide the caring role. A clear priority is to gain a better understanding of the needs of these children and young people, and their kinship carers through research and appropriate and culturally responsive service developments.

5.1 Identified issues

Based on the professionals' contribution in this study, a number of key issues impacting on orphans and their kinship carers were identified. These included both groups having insufficient financial and other resources; inadequate accommodation; emotional/psychological issues; cultural complexities; resettlement issues; and uncertainty about rights and obligations under Australian law. It is important to recognise that, as the literature suggests, some of these issues mirror those experienced by kinship carers generally. For example, kinship carers often have limited socio-economic resources and the placement of a new child or young person with the family brings with it substantial financial burdens. The existing housing capacity may not be suitable and the new child/young person coming into the family may change family relationships with other children and the parents. However, the study also identifies a number of issues that are unique to the experience of international kinship care. For example, there are significant cultural complexities for the children settling in a new country and the 'culture shock' of having to live in a completely new environment with different laws, social arrangements and customs. Children and young people often have substantial histories of trauma through war and conflict and the loss of close relatives such as parents, in addition to the stressors arising from the transition process itself when they come to live in Australia. Taking these issues together, the study suggests that Orphan Relative Visa holders and their carers in Australia are likely to experience a similar range of issues as other kinship care arrangements, but with an added layer of complexity associated with cultural and resettlement issues.

Summary

The key issues impacting on Orphan Relative Visa holders and their carers include:

- Lack of financial and other resources and the stress of meeting various competing needs presented by the placement of the child/young person with the host family
- Accommodation related problems including a lack of living and sleeping space with associated possible overcrowding and a lack of privacy
- The necessary level of preparation for the resettlement process and dealing with unrealistic expectations of children/young people and carers

- Potential culture shock for the child/young person moving into a new culture and related misunderstandings and misinterpretations of actions and behaviours

- Difficulties and uncertainty about rights and obligations under Australian law system both in relation to the migration/visa process and more generally

- For kinship carers, a range of issues related to the caring role including limited knowledge about available services and supports and/or difficulties accessing services and supports; securing the necessary resources to support the newly placed child/young person; and, skills and knowledge to deal with behavioural, settlement and other issues experienced by the child/young person

- For the child/young person a range of issues related to the migration process including dealing with histories of trauma and loss, potential exposure to racism and culture shock and the general difficulties fitting into a new life in a new country.

Recommendations

In relation to the identified issues for Orphan Relative Visa holders and their carers, specific recommendations include:

1. That there is recognition in both policy and service provision that children/young people and their carers in international kinship care placements are likely to experience a similar range of issues to other kinship/foster care placements.

2. That there is recognition in both policy and service provision that the resettlement process has inherent and unique difficulties that give international kinship care arrangements an added layer of complexity, particularly challenges for children/young people settling into a new culture.

5.2 Needs

This study also identified a range of specific needs related to the issues identified for children/young people and their carers. These needs were related to an array of key areas that include finance/resources, accommodation/housing, emotional/psychological wellbeing, culture and the resettlement process. While many of the identified needs are tangible, practical needs such as having adequate income to support children, others are more complex such as the need for specialist mental health treatment for children and young people with significant histories of trauma. As with the issues identified in this study, many of the needs are common to all kinship care/foster care placements, while some are unique to international kinship care. It is important that these children and their kinship carers receive similar levels of support and resources to other kinship care arrangements in Australia, as well as recognition of the specific additional needs that arise from the international migration process.

Summary

The key needs of Orphan Relative Visa holders and their carers identified in this study include:

- The need for the carer family to have sufficient financial resources from employment, social security and other sources to cover additional expenses related to the placement including day-to-day living expenses, health and education expenses, and social/recreational expenses.
- Because young people who arrive on orphan visas often have no access to any source of independent income (such as Youth Allowance) for at least two years, they lack the ability to buy personal items, school/study related items and money for leisure activities.
- Carer families need access to affordable, adequate housing that is large enough to accommodate the extra child/young person adequately, a crucial factor in any successful re-settlement.
- The resettlement process often impacts on the emotional/psychological health of children/young people and their carers, and both frequently need access to social and emotional support, and at times to specialist mental health services. Information on the availability of these services is thus vital.

- In relation to the cultural aspects of the resettlement process, children and young people need assistance and time to settle in a new culture. This means having the capacity and opportunity to maintain and develop links with their own culture, a culturally sensitive and supportive home environment, and support and opportunity to develop a new cultural and personal identity in Australia if they so wish.
- Both children/young people and carers have a range of needs directly related to the re-settlement process including information on the process and on services/supports prior to migration, assistance to avoid unreasonable expectations (by the child/young person or carer), preparation for difficulties that may occur and clarity about legal rights and responsibilities.

Recommendations

In relation to the identified needs of Orphan Relative Visa holders and their carers, specific recommendations include:

1. That carers/families taking on an international kinship care role be adequately resourced (financial and other) to perform the care role, and that the particular extra financial costs of international migration processes for children/young people are made clear.
2. Because adequate housing is critical for the success of the resettlement process, that carers/host families must receive access to accommodation/housing that is suitable for the kinship caring role.
3. That there is recognition that significant emotional/psychological impacts are inherent in the migration and resettlement process and thus children/young people and their carers need access to a range of practical and emotional supports and more specialised mental health services.
4. That there is recognition that children/young people and their carers may require assistance with a range of practical and cultural issues associated with the international migration experience and the resettlement process.

5.3 Supports

One of the strongest themes to emerge from the study is the need for improved and coordinated supports for children/young people and their carers during the critical settlement phase, a period of up to 12 months following arrival in Australia. There is an apparent tension between the extent to which such support services should focus on risk identification as opposed to purely providing support. However, what is clear is that these services should be culturally appropriate, recognising the diverse backgrounds and experiences of the Orphan Relative Visa holders and their kinship carers. The support function would also need to be flexible, recognising that in some settlement situations the carer and children/young people might need little more than information on services and supports available (including government services such as Centrelink and Medicare) and the contact details should problems arise. In contrast, some situations will require more direct support and ongoing case management. Some form of financial support, either as a direct payment/grant to families or via a support organisation may also be a useful option to examine given that many of the needs and issues for kinship carers relate to the financial, housing and other resources required for the placements. A key consideration is also when support services should commence and for how long after arrival they should be provided. Some research participants argued that initial support contacts should occur prior to the child's/young person's arrival. This would allow carer families to secure a relationship with crucial services and supports prior to any issues developing. Given the type of services to be provided, the support function would most suitably sit with a NGO. Such an organisation is more likely to be able to build trust with the key communities where the majority of Orphan Relative Visa holders come from, rather than a statutory agency with more formal functions that government departments are required to perform. There was also a view that, at minimum, international kinship care placements should have similar levels of formal support provision as is found with other types of placement such as international adoption and foster/kinship care placements within Australia.

Summary

The main points about supports for Orphan Relative Visa holders and their carers identified in this study include:

- Strong agreement that there should be support services to assist children/young people and carers in the resettlement process.
- Providing adequate supports should be seen as a key to preventing the breakdown of placements.
- Supports are needed in a range of areas from practical aspects (such as financial support and information provision) through to more formalised counselling and case management.
- Whatever model of support is provided, a crucial requirement is that it be provided in a culturally appropriate and sensitive way.
- Support functions should ideally be based within a non-government organisation experienced in providing culturally sensitive services and which has the capacity to link to a broader range of community based support services and, where necessary, statutory services.

Recommendations

In relation to the supports for Orphan Relative Visa holders and their carers specific recommendations include:

1. That there is development of specialised support services to assist international kinship care placements during the resettlement process.

2. That the importance of providing support for the resettlement process is recognised as a primary strategy to prevent placement breakdown.

3. That at minimum, supports for orphan relative placements should be at least comparable to other in fostering and adoption, and should recognise the particular complexities of the international migration process.

5.4 System improvements

While there was strong agreement amongst participants in this study that the key improvement required in the service system is a specific support service function for the Orphan Relative Visa program, the extent to which these services should have an assessment and risk management function was debated. Most participants thought such a service should be primarily a culturally appropriate support service that was accessed voluntarily and focused on making carers and children aware of the available supports and services. Moreover, it should where necessary, undertake a case management role which links the orphans and carers into the other services. While this model would focus primarily on support, it could also identify and respond to any risk issues in a supportive way and, where necessary, report them to relevant statutory authorities. A counterview held by a smaller proportion of participants argued for such a service to have a strong assessment function (both prior to placement to assess carer suitability and then ongoing as a risk management strategy). It should be noted that such a disagreement is not unique to the international kinship care context, and as presented in the literature review, the issue of risk management versus support has been a major area of debate in the broader out-of-home-care/foster care field. In practice, most participants rejected a simple 'one-off snap shot' assessment of suitability – whether prior to placement to assess suitability, or after placement to assess ongoing suitability – as an ineffective approach that would have a major impact on building trust and engaging with carer families. Most desired a primarily supportive function that began prior to the child's/young person's arrival, that was voluntary, and that also, as part of the ongoing work, would allow the monitoring of risks and, if necessary, referral to statutory authorities.

A further issue is whether matching the suitability of potential carers for particular children/young people should happen first as a condition of the visa granting process. Most participants in the study strongly rejected this approach. By their very nature, these children and young people often come from particularly dire circumstances having lost parents and other family/supports. Further, the potential relative carers are also often recent arrivals in Australia with experience of significant disadvantage. A standard approach utilising assessments employed in other fostering contexts may determine a potential placement as high risk without recognising that the placement may be the best option available considering the very difficult situation. Most professionals preferred an approach that was primarily supportive, that helped both carer and child/young person during the migration process and, hence, that would enable problems to be detected early and addressed immediately, and which would act on risk issues only if they arise.

Summary

The main points in relation to service system improvements for Orphan Relative Visa holders and their carers identified in this study include:

- There is strong agreement on the need for an improvement in the provision of support services, although views differ on the extent to which such support services should have assessment and risk management functions.
- The major view was that 'one off' assessments of suitability (either pre or post arrival of the child/young person) would be ineffective and rather that assessment should be part of the ongoing development of a working relationship with families.
- There was little support for mandatory assessments of suitability to be undertaken as a precursor to the granting of visas.

Recommendations

In relation to service system improvements for Orphan Relative Visa holders and their carers, specific recommendations include:

1. That there is development of specialised support services for orphan international kinship care placements.

2. That 'one off' assessments of suitability, either pre or post granting of visas, is not supported as a preferred model.

3. That the preferred service system response would be a specialised and culturally sensitive support service able to work with children/young people and their kinship carers in an ongoing way from prior to migration and according to need, with the capacity to link to other services including statutory protection services where required.

5.5 Overall recommendations

Based on the findings and key conclusions drawn from this study, the following overall recommendations are made:

1. That there be greater recognition of the issues and needs of Orphan Relative Visa holders and their carers in government policy and associated service provision.

2. That service provision and support services for Orphan Relative Visa holders and their carers should recognise the specific support needs arising from the international migration process and subsequent settlement issues in Australia.

3. That a specific support service for Orphan Relative Visas holders and their carers be funded and established in one or more non-government organisations with the capacity to provide culturally appropriate family support and case management services.

4. That the orientation of support services established for the Orphan Relative Visa program primarily be support and resourcing functions to maximise the likelihood that placements will continue rather than services being focussed primarily on assessing suitability and managing risk.

References

AIHW. (2015). *Child protection Australia: 2013–14*. Australian Institute of Health and Welfare. Canberra: AIHW.

Australian Government (2014). 'Settlement Database: Settlers with Visa Subclass of 117 - State of Residence then Gender then Age on Arrival then Country of Birth - 01 July 2012 to 04 November 2014', Canberra: Department of Social Services.

Boetto, H. (2010). 'Kinship Care: A review of issues.' *Family Matters*, 85: 60–67.

Breman, R. (2014). 'Peeling back the layers – kinship care in Victoria.' Camberwell: Baptcare.

Brown, L. & Sen, R. (2014). 'Improving outcomes for looked after children: A critical analysis of kinship care.' *Practice: Social Work in Action*, (3) 161–180.

Bryman, A. (2008). *Social Research Methods*, 3rd ed., Oxford: Oxford University Press.

Cardoso, J., Gomez, R., & Padilla, Y. (2009). 'What Happens When Family Resources Are Across International Boundaries? An Exploratory Study on Kinship Placements in Mexican Immigrant Families.' *Child Welfare*, 88(6): 67–84.

Department of Families, Housing, Community Services and Indigenous Affairs. (2011). *An outline of the standards for out-of-home-care*. Canberra: Commonwealth of Australia.

Dunne, E. G. & Kettler, L. J. (2008). 'Social and emotional issues of children in kinship foster care and stressors on kinship carers: A review of the Australian and international literature.' *Children Australia*, 31 (2), 22–28.

Farmer, E. (2010). 'What factors relate to good placement outcomes in kinship care?' *British Journal of Social Work*, 40: 426–444.

Freundlich, M., Heffernan, M. & Jacobs, J. (2004) 'Interjurisdictional placement of children in foster care.' *Child Welfare*, 83(1): 5–26.

Kavanagh, S. (2013). *Home Safe Home: A report on children who migrate to Australia for kinship care*. Melbourne: International Social Service Australia.

Kavanagh, S. (2011). *International Kinship Care: Observations from the Australian context*. Melbourne: International Social Service Australia.

Naughton, D., & Fay, K. (2003). 'Of kin and culture: US children and international kinship care placements.' *Adoption & Fostering*, 27(4): 30–37.

Northcott, F., & Jeffries, W. (2013). 'Forgotten families: international family connections for children in the American public child-welfare system.' *Family Law Quarterly*, *47*(2): 273–298.

Northcott, F., & Jeffries, W. (2012). 'Family finding and engagement beyond the bench: Working across international borders. *Juvenile & Family Court Journal*, 63(1): 31–47.

O'Brien, V. (2014). 'Responding to the call: a conceptual model for kinship care assessment.' *Child and Family Social Work*, 19: 355–366.

Oien, C. (2006). 'Transnational networks of care: Angolan children in fosterage in Portugal.' *Ethnic And Racial Studies*, 29(6): 1104–1117.

Palacious, J. & Jimenez, J. (2009) 'Kinship foster care protection or risk?' *Adoption and Fostering*, 33(3): 64–75.

Paxman, M. (2006). *Outcomes for children and young people in kinship care: An issues paper*. Ashfield, NSW: NSW Department of Community Services.

Queensland Child Safety Services. (undated). *Kinship care: A literature review.* Brisbane: Queensland Government Department of Communities.

Roby, J. (2011). *Children in informal alternative care discussion paper.* New York: UNICEF.

Strozier , A. L. (2012). 'The effectiveness of support groups in increasing social support for kinship caregivers.' *Children and Youth Services Review*, 34, 876–881.

Tarren-Sweeney, M. (2013). 'An investigation of complex attachment- and trauma-related symptomatology among children in foster and kinship care.' *Child Psychiatry and Human Development*, 44, 727–741.

Wichinsky, L., Thomas, J., Dejohn, T. & Turney, H. (2013). 'Identifying unmet needs: Recommendations for creating a model of kinship subsidy program.' *Journal of Family Social Work*, 16, 431–446.

Wilson, A., Enawalla, M. & Navey, J. (2014). *International kinship care: Trends, challenges and outcomes for children placed with family overseas.* London: Children and Families Across Borders (CFAB).

Winokur, M., Holtan, A., & Batchelder , K. (2014). 'Kinship care for the safety, permanency, and well-being of children removed from the home for maltreatment.' *Cochrane Database Of Systematic Reviews 2014*, Issue 1.

Valle, J. & Bravo, A. (2013). 'Current trends, figures and challenges in out of home child care: An international comparative analysis.' *Psychosocial Intervention,* 22:251-257.

Victorian Department of Human Services. (2009) *A New Kinship Care Program Model for Victoria*. Melbourne: Victorian Department of Human Services.

Yardley, A., Mason, J. & Watson, E. (2009). *Kinship Care in NSW: Finding a way forward.* Bankstown: University of Western Sydney.

www.ingramcontent.com/pod-product-compliance
Ingram Content Group Australia Pty Ltd
76 Discovery Rd, Dandenong South VIC 3175, AU
AUHW020134130726
429791AU00003B/135

9 781925 333497